Writers & Their Contexts

Series editor John Spiers, Senior Research Fellow,
Institute of English Studies, School of Advanced Study,
University of London

1. John Sutherland, *The Secret Trollope: Anthony Trollope Uncovered*.
2. Edward Guiliano, *Lewis Carroll: The Worlds of His Alices*.
3. Albert Rolls, *Thomas Pynchon: The Demon in the Text*.
4. Jo Brantley Berryman, *Ezra Pound's Aesthetics and The Origins of Modernism*.
5. Terence Bareham, *George Crabbe: The Hidden Self of Nature's Sternest Painter*.

WRITERS & THEIR CONTEXTS
No. 3

THOMAS PYNCHON
The Demon in the Text

Thomas Pynchon
The Demon in the Text

by
Albert Rolls

EER
Edward Everett Root Publishers, Brighton, 2019

For Raquel and For Dionisio

EER
Edward Everett Root, Publishers, Co. Ltd.,
30 New Road, Brighton, Sussex, BN1 1BN, England.
www.eerpublishing.com

edwardeverettroot@yahoo.co.uk

Thomas Pynchon
The Demon in the Text

Albert Rolls

Writers and Their Contexts series, No.3.

ISBN: 978-1-912224-54-8 Hardback
ISBN: 978-1-912224-55-5 Paperback
ISBN: 978-1-912224-56-2 eBook

© Albert Rolls 2019

The rights of the author have been asserted under the Copyright, Designs and Patents Act 1998 as the owner of this work.

All rights reserved. No part of this publication may be reproduced, stored in a retrieval system or transmitted, in any form or by any means, electronic, mechanical, photocopying, recording or otherwise, without the prior permission of the copyright owner.

Illustration on front cover is 'The Abstract Flag', an original painting by Ashlie Miller.

Designed by Pageset Limited, High Wycombe, Buckinghamshire.
Printed in Great Britain by Lightning Source UK, Milton Keynes.

CONTENTS

ACKNOWLEDGEMENTS
IX

NOTE ON THE TEXT
XI

FICTIONAL AUTOBIOGRAPHIES AND
AUTOBIOGRAPHICAL FICTIONS
1

"A DUAL MAN [AND OEUVRE], AIMED TWO WAYS AT ONCE":
THE TWO DIRECTIONS OF PYNCHON'S LIFE AND THOUGHT
21

CONSIDERING THE ENCLAVE
71

EPILOGUE
99

ENDNOTES
101

BIBLIOGRAPHY
137

Index
153

Acknowledgements

This book brings together for the first time new material and revisions of work that has appeared in article form. A version of "Fictional Autobiographies and Autobiographical Fictions" was published in *Orbit: Writing around Pynchon* 1:2 (2013) under the title "Thomas Pynchon and the Vacuum Salesman in Guadalajara." The present version of the chapter incorporates, along with new material, part of "Pynchon, In His Absence," *Orbit: Writing around Pynchon* 1:1 (2012), and a rewritten version of a blog post (April 6, 2015)—the revision of which Nassau County's adding historical maps to its Website facilitated—that appeared on *Queen Mob's Tea House*, the founding editor of which, Russell Bennetts, was kind enough to give me an opportunity to blog, a task I did not pursue with the conscientiousness that I should have. A shorter version of "'A Dual Man [and Oeuvre], Aimed Two Ways at Once': The Two Directions of Pynchon's Life and Thought" appeared in *Orbit: Writing around Pynchon* 4:1 (2016) and integrates material from my review of *Bleeding Edge* in *Orbit: Writing around Pynchon* 2:1 (2013) as well as from "*Inherent Vice*'s Two Directions," which first appeared in *Berfrois* (February 13, 2014). "Considering the Enclave" is built upon a portion of an article on Pynchon's letters and juvenilia that appears in *Pynchon in Context* (Cambridge University Press). The material, considerably expanded, is repurposed here in accordance with the terms of the agreement I signed with Cambridge UP. Finally, Note 92 appeared in *Orbit* 5:2 (2017) as "Pynchon's Creative Misuse of Entropy" with a response, some of the elements of which I address in the version here, from David Letzler, and Note 78, since updated, appeared as "Thomas Pynchon & Kirkpatrick Sale – Their Unfinished Science Fiction Musical 'Minstrel Island'" on http://thomaspynchon.com, the always useful Website run by Tim Ware, who needs to be thanked for other help that he provided.

    Among the people who have helped me as I worked on this book, John Krafft deserves the most thanks. He has been an overly generous sounding board, responding to questions and reading drafts of papers, including a thorough reading of a near final draft of the entire manuscript. He has pointed me in better directions more times than I can properly recall. David Ramm, on the strength of a biographical article that I wrote for *World Authors, 2000–2005* (2007), gave me a contract for a book on Pynchon that I never managed to pull together, but the possibility of its being published gave me the freedom to pursue my research. This book serves as a replacement; I hope it meets his approval. Martin Eve, the founding editor of *Orbit*, greeted my submissions with more enthusiasm than they possibly deserved, simultaneously encouraging me to continue with and rework the material that I wanted to believe had been complete when I first gave it to him. Sascha Pöhlmann patiently read revisions of the draft of "The Two Directions of Pynchon's Life and Thought" as I played with it, not always reasonably given its need at the time to stand alone, in preparation for its appearance in *Orbit*, and Inger H. Dalsgaard offered some helpful comments on text that discusses Pynchon's letters. Luc Herman and Jonathan Glassow provided access to material they had gathered on their own but had not made public. Their generosity allowed me to fill in gaps that otherwise would have remained. Finally, Frances Louis, who has been a friend for almost thirty years, read through the entire manuscript, offering advice on style. Any infelicities that remain are the result of my ear's lacking the grace her ear, as well as Krafft's, possesses. The book could not have been written without the indulgence of Raquel Rolls, my wife, who gave up vacation time so that I could visit libraries and allowed our household budget to be reduced so that I could buy books.

Note on the Text

Parenthetical citations are used throughout, including in the endnotes. The letters to and from Corlies Smith are from *Of a Fond Ghoul* (1990). The book lacks page numbers, so the letters' dates are used for citation purposes.

All citations from Pynchon's works are from the first U.S. editions with the exception of those from *V.* I use the first British edition of that novel for reasons that my "The Two *V.*s of Thomas Pynchon, or From Lippincott to Jonathan Cape and Beyond" (*Orbit: Writing around Pynchon.* 1:1 [2012]) makes clear.

The following abbreviations for Pynchon's works are used:

CL49	*The Crying of Lot 49*
"JMW"	"Journey into the Mind of Watts"
GR	*Gravity's Rainbow*
SL	*Slow Learner*
Vl	*Vineland*
M&D	*Mason & Dixon*
AtD	*Against the Day*
IV	*Inherent Vice*
BE	*Bleeding Edge*

In the discussion of "Minstrel Island," P is placed in parenthetical citations when it is necessary to distinguish Pynchon's contributions to the musical from those of Kirkpatrick Sale, whose contributions are flagged with an S in parentheses when appropriate.

I should also note that I have not used "sic" for errors, nor corrected those errors, in quotations from Pynchon's letters. They were written informally, a quality that ought to be respected.

Fictional Autobiographies and Autobiographical Fictions

IN the essay "Hallowe'en? Over Already?" (1999), Thomas Pynchon writes about some of the fall 1998 goings on at the Cathedral School in New York City, where his son, Jackson, was enrolled in the second grade. They included a picnic[1]; the Blessing of the Animals, which the Pynchons missed that year as they had the year before, at the church associated with the school, the Cathedral of Saint John the Divine; and a field trip to the Tenafly Nature Center, where the second grade observed and were observed by a giant bullfrog, compensation "(sort of)" for missing the elephant's yearly appearance at the Blessing.[2] Pynchon goes on to recall an "impromptu tour" (1) of the Cathedral that he and his son, along with a number of other children, were treated to the previous year. Under Pynchon's eye and the children's curiosity, which had been awakened by the enthusiasm of their tour guide, Gina Bria Vescovi, the church becomes a site of both actual and imaginative exploration, as if it were "a sinister and wonderful Card Table which exhibits the cheaper Wave-like Grain known in the Trade as Wand'ring Heart, causing an illusion of Depth into which for years children have gaz'd as into the illustrated Pages of Books" (*M&D* 5).

The children's gazes, of course, had objects less illusionary to explore at the Cathedral than those that can be projected into an eccentric eighteenth-century wood grain. The highlights include "organ consoles, amplifiers, hiding places," and a "Pentecostal profusion of mini-chapels" (3). The chapels, the guide reveals, were incorporated into the building—the "'original core'" of which "'was an orphanage, in the oldest and best sense, a place for people who had nowhere else to go'" (3)—for the benefit of newcomers who were arriving in the city during the church's construction, something that ties the architecture of the building to the history of the United States, particularly "the great wave of immigration" (3) around the turn of the century. The setting isn't completely lacking in illusion: lest we mistake the scene's interest as simply factual, Pynchon draws his readers' attention to the nave that seems high enough to accommodate the Statue of Liberty, presumably from the children's perspective—although the reference to Lady Liberty connects Pynchon's interest in the Cathedral's hospitable place in the history of immigration to the children's wonder—and to a stained-glass window that depicts the Titanic in which the children search for Leonardo DiCaprio. This search is perhaps another reference to the United States' immigrant past, for DiCaprio's character in *Titanic* (1997) could serve as a representative of those who died on their journeys and whose histories, therefore, are absent from the Cathedral's. Pynchon then turns his focus to spiral staircases that wind up into shadows inaccessible to the public and about which the knowledgeable guide will say nothing except that we wouldn't believe what was up there. More questioning on Pynchon's part merely elicits the guide's mild laughter.

Pynchon is looking forward to revisiting, along with the children, the Cathedral for another tour. Maybe this time he'll get upstairs, but "with Hallowe'en coming" (3) that might not be the best idea. What's there? That becomes the question. Playing off the Cathedral tradition of showing classic horror movies during Hallowe'en week and an apparent rumor that a bishop's ghost haunts the pews—which may be an allusion to the spectacle of "a giant ghost rising from the august tomb of Bishop William Manning" (Bell) that was an element of the yearly holiday festivities that accompanied the film festival—Pynchon offers the possibility of bats, "*vampire* bats" (3), or strange people swinging on bell ropes. He concludes by wondering if he should wear his son's Darth Vader costume from the previous year and carry its "light," with new batteries "just in case" (3).

This rare autobiographical essay, written for the sole delight of the Cathedral School community—though it is hard to imagine that Pynchon wasn't resigned to having copies find their way onto the collector's market—provides a model, perhaps the best one available at present, for fashioning a biography of Pynchon. One is obliged, after all, to "*project a world*" or "[i]f not project then at least flash some arrow on the dome to skitter among constellations and trace out your Dragon, Whale, Southern Cross" (*CL49* 82), even if one also takes part in a metaphorical quest—as Mathew Winston characterizes the process of researching his early biographical essay—analogous to the one Stencil is on in *V.* (1963). The biographer approaches Pynchon's life much as Pynchon approaches the Cathedral and the shadows above its spiraled staircases and the space beyond—or the children the objects they come across, particularly the stained-glass picture of the Titanic, a representative example, the reader assumes—developing a text from available information, whether it derives from rumor or more substantial sources. The question one is left asking is not only What is there to be found? but also What shape can be traced over the clusters of information that one finds?

Consider, for example, the Pynchon anecdotes told by the television producer Deane Rink—who attended Cornell a few years after Pynchon and studied creative writing under Walter Slatoff, with whom Pynchon had also studied. Rink tells his stories as part of an early Web exercise in which he sent emails for publication to the *B&R Samizdat Express* at the end of 1996, when he was in McMurdo, Antarctica, to work on *Live from Antarctica* (1997) for PBS Productions. Discussing mostly literary figures, Rink turns to Pynchon and the origin of "Mortality and Mercy in Vienna" (1959), which Rink initially mistakes for "Under the Rose" (1961), an error he asks to have corrected in a subsequent email. Claiming Slatoff as his source, Rink writes that in order to ignite an otherwise desultory creative writing class, Slatoff put "a random sentence on the board and ask[ed] everybody in class to start off with that sentence and write for the whole hour. Pynchon refused to turn his paper in at hour's end, but walked across the hall to the English Dept. office and continued to scribble away for another hour. He finally finished the story: it was subsequently published in *Epoch* [...and] was anthologized in the *Best Short Stories* of whatever year that was" (Rink).

The anecdote is fascinating, but even if one ignores the confusion over which short story Rink is discussing and which one appeared in *Best American Short Stories*,[3] one remains unsure of its value as biographical fact. Rink is ad libbing to impress an audience—as Slatoff may well have done to inspire a desultory class in which Rink participated—with what he hopes will be accepted as insider knowledge, something further illustrated by his "revelation" that while *V.* was Pynchon's first published novel, *The Crying of Lot 49* (1966) was the first to be written, an assertion that leaves one wondering whether Rink had read the second novel, which contains references that clearly place its time of composition after *V.*'s publication, or, if he had read it, whether he remembered it. Rink further reveals his desire to impress when he recalls, "Rumor was that he [Pynchon] was offered an instant professorship upon graduation, but turned it down to sell vacuum cleaners in Guadalajara," where Dick Schaap reported Pynchon was living in 1964 (6). The professorship is an embellished characterization of the Wilson Fellowship that Pynchon was offered. It would have obliged him to teach, but he turned it down to focus on his writing. The vacuum-salesman business, by contrast, is obvious fiction, mentioned for its surprise value and perhaps to evince Pynchon's mysteriousness by leading us to ask, What do we really know about his life? The story also raises a different kind of question, even if Rink never asserts it is true: Whose story is it, Rink's or the Cornell rumor mill's of the mid-sixties, when, the context suggests, it circulated? Without corroboration from another student of the period, one isn't inclined to take Rink at his word, but the problem turns out to be more complicated than one would at first imagine.

That wild rumors about Pynchon circulated on the Cornell campus in the 1960s is certainly believable. Even before he became a novelist, John Diebold and Michael Goodwin— both Cornell students in the early 1960s—tell us, Pynchon was a subject of discussion at Cornell, "a well-known campus character, respected as much for his adventures with Cornell Folk Song Club president Richard Fariña as for his writing abilities."[4] The vacuum-salesman story could simply be one of the rumors. Rink, however, isn't the only one to relate a story about Pynchon being a vacuum salesman, and the source for another one has nothing to do with Cornell campus conjecture. In a review of the Swiss filmmakers Donatello and Fosco Dubini's *Journey into the Mind of [P.]* (2002), Ron Silliman recalls Mimi Baez-Fariña, Fariña's widow, telling him in the early seventies, before the appearance of *Gravity's Rainbow* (1973), that "Pynchon was [. . .] selling vacuum cleaners door to door, having exhausted his earnings as a writer," though Silliman adds, "It was hard to envision then & I still don't know if Mimi was teasing me."

Rink could have picked up the notion that Pynchon was a vacuum salesman from someplace other than Cornell—from someone else that Mimi or another member of Pynchon's circle misinformed or from a source further removed—forgotten where he heard the story, and assumed he must have done so while he was in college. Pynchon or someone in his circle of friends could also have heard about the Cornell rumor and decided it would be amusing to spread it beyond the campus community, altering some of its elements to furnish it with an air of credibility, however slight. Other possibilities for where the story originated are imaginable: it is even plausible that Pynchon had something to do with Mimi's answering inquiries about her late husband's friend with the absurd notion—that he had provided her with a story to relate. At the beginning of his career, he had provided another friend with an absurd tale to pass on, telling Faith Sale, whom he knew from college and who went on to become an editor, including for Pynchon, that in the event any reporters called her in search of information about him, she should "either (a) tell them nothing at all, or (b) better, tell them something far out, like I am a Negro living in Ft. Wayne with my grandmother and keeping her in narcotics by working as a freelance jobber in auto accessories. And very fat, though I subsist on nothing but saki and raw Brussels sprouts" (June 2, 1963).

If his suggestion to Faith Sale or his considering telling *Who's Who* "that he was born in Mexico, that his parents were Irving Pynchon and Guadalupe Ibarguengotia and that he was 'named Exotic Dancers Man of the Year in 1957' and 'regional coordinator for the March of Edsel Owners on Washington (MEOW) in 1961'" (Gussow) is any indication, Pynchon has toyed throughout his career with the possibilities his approach to publicity offered. And he, at least occasionally, has taken on a role similar to the one Ms. Vescovi assumes on the Cathedral tour when dealing with the space above the spiral stairs, that is, serving as the unforthcoming, amused guide. For instance, he wrote or is alleged to have written to the *Soho Weekly News* to say "Not bad, keep trying" (quoted in Tony Tanner 18), after it published, in 1976, John Calvin Batchelor's "Thomas Pynchon Is Not Thomas Pynchon," an article in which Batchelor claimed "Thomas Pynchon" was a pseudonym that J. D. Salinger had assumed.[5] In 2004, Pynchon voiced a caricature of himself on *The Simpsons* (1989–), making fun of his reputation for reclusiveness: "Hey, over here! Have your picture taken with a reclusive author! Today only, we'll throw in a free autograph! But wait, there's more!" In 2013, he, at the very least, authorized having a character nicknamed Sleazus in the book trailer for *Bleeding Edge* (2013) wear a t-shirt that says, "Hi, I'm Tom Pynchon" (see http://thomaspynchon.com/pynchon-media/), and allowed Penguin to produce a t-shirt to promote the novel that says, "Hi I'm Thomas Pynchon." He was also rumored to have made a cameo in Paul Thomas Anderson's 2014 adaptation of *Inherent Vice* (2009), turning the experience of the film, at least for certain viewers, into something of a *Where's-Waldo* game. Josh Brolin, who plays Bigfoot, seemed to confirm the rumor, observing, "'I don't think anybody knew' Mr. Pynchon was on the set. [...] 'He came on as the kind of mercurial iconoclast he is. He stayed in the corner'" (Wickman).[6] A doctor in the cafeteria of the Chryskylodon facility emerged as a likely contender for Pynchon, but that doctor turned out to be Charley Morgan, a character actor and apparent friend of Anderson who said, "There's no Thomas Pynchon cameo. Not at all. [...] I talked to Paul Anderson about it" (Daly).

Beyond his early short stories, novels, and the occasional nonfiction pieces, Pynchon has more often addressed the public with silence—nonetheless insisting in a 1978 letter to Candida Donadio, "As for spilling my life story, I try to do that all the time" (Gussow). The record has, as a result, become colored by "gossip about girlfriends, drug use, favorite TV programs and pig fetishes, and trivia about eating habits and clothing preferences" (12), as John Krafft writes. The portrait of Pynchon that the biographer can sketch is, therefore, a mixture of rumor and fact, both of which are parts of the story of the public figure Pynchon has simultaneously become and avoided being and thus are important to understanding the idea of Thomas Pynchon. The Dubinis' approach Pynchon from such a perspective, the bracketed "P." of their film's title representing not so much Pynchon as the collective body of those who have taken to fashioning stories around his absence and who often, for example on the Pynchon e-mail list, use the shorthand "P" for his name. The film is intent on illustrating the semi-fictional nature of its P., calling attention to contradictions that are a product of the lack of a public story about Pynchon: text that flashes on the screen, for example, states that Pynchon's whereabouts and marital status are unknown shortly before the now inactive Pynchomane Richard Lane mentions Pynchon's wife and child and the London *Times's* James Bone discusses his finding out in the late nineties where Pynchon lives via the Internet. Truth is in some cases beside the point. The late Stephen Tomaske reveals that his interest in pursuing his biographical research was spurred by his being told an "urban legend" concerning Pynchon, a tale about his hiding inside a casket to avoid photographers while getting into Bob Dylan's wedding. Lane, near the movie's beginning, thus posits that there are two Pynchons, the private man who "drinks his coffee" in the morning, a characterization that is, paradoxically, a conjecture on Lane's part, and the figure who inhabits the minds of his cultish fans.[7]

Pynchon seems to have obliquely played with the two-Pynchons idea when John Larroquette sent him for review the script of "Newcomer," the December 7, 1993, episode of *The John Larroquette Show* in which references to Pynchon play a part. In the episode, Daryl Mitchell's character, Dexter Walker, who operates the lunch counter in the St. Louis bus station where the show is set, casually remarks to Larroquette's character, John Hemingway, that he is friends with Pynchon, whom Hemingway admires. After looking at the script, Pynchon, through his agent and wife, Melanie Jackson, told Don Reo, the show's creator and head writer, that the script calls "him Tom, and no one ever calls him Tom" (Sales 63), which the evidence suggests those on first-name terms with him do call him. Those who don't generally call him "Tom," we can assume, are outside his circle of family, friends, and publishing contacts. Pynchon seems to have wanted the Pynchon figure mentioned on the show to refer not to Tom, the physical person, but to Pynchon as idea, which would explain why "Pynchon refused [. . .] to let a *Larroquette* extra, in a plaid shirt, be videotaped from the rear and represent Pynchon. 'He asked us not to pretend he was in the environment at all,' Larroquette said" (Williams). The discussion of Pynchon on the show is therefore confined to an earlier presence—his appearance the previous night, when he visited Dexter, wearing, it is said, a t-shirt bearing an image of Roky Ericson, the musician who Pynchon requested be mentioned instead of Willy Deville as the script had originally called for—and his work, an imaginary novel that Pynchon asked to have called *Pandemonium of the Sun*, a phrase taken from Cormac McCarthy's *Blood Meridian* (1985). "In a weird way," Larroquette remarked, "we got him [Pynchon] to rewrite the script" (Williams), transforming it, we might add, into an allegory of his biography.

To divide Tom the man from Pynchon the idea for biographical purposes, however, is to risk the folly in which Lane indulges in *Journey into the Mind of [P.]*, particularly when he speculates that Pynchon was on the bus Lee Harvey Oswald took from Houston, Texas, to Mexico City on September 26, 1963,[8] about a month after Pynchon served as best man at

Richard Fariña and Mimi Baez's wedding on August 21, 1963. Lane never offers an explanation for why Pynchon would travel from California to Texas to return to Mexico rather than take a bus from Pacific Grove, to which he had traveled from Mexico City in August (see Hajdu 178–79; Kachka 52). Lane admits that he is offering nothing more than "ridiculous rumor," a description he recasts as "ridiculous speculation," apparently to indicate that the story is his own, but he also conjectures that Pynchon's "secret," his reason for avoiding the press, involves the conversation he had with Oswald. "This is the kind of fun people like me can have," Lane then says. But the speculation isn't simply ridiculous; it ignores the record, even as it existed at the time of the film's making. Pynchon had already begun his famed avoidance of the media before Oswald went to Mexico, as George Plimpton, a literary journalist, and Jules Siegel, a former friend, point out in the film just after Lane's speculation. There is no reasonable way to place Pynchon on a bus with Oswald, despite Lane's insistence that connections can be forged even if the words we have don't imply them, or to attribute Pynchon's desire for privacy to a meeting between him and John F. Kennedy's assassin. Indeed, it has more recently been revealed that Pynchon headed further north after Fariña's wedding, going to Seattle and then Oregon (see To Hillock, 1964), where he likely saw his college friend David Shetzline (To Kirkpatrick and Faith Sale, March 27, 1964), before meeting up with Mary Ann Tharaldsen and David Seidler—Cornell friends with whom he stayed when he arrived in Seattle to work for Boeing in 1960—in Berkeley, where he remained until "shortly after ... Kennedy was assassinated" (Kachka 52).[9]

But even in the absence of information about Pynchon's whereabouts after Fariña's wedding, there would be little need to construct a foundational myth to explain Pynchon's avoidance of the press. Pynchon had gained a reputation for keeping to himself even before journalists were interested in pursuing him, something demonstrated by a 1961 internal Lippincott memo, dated July 10, a photocopy of which is reprinted in *Of a Fond Ghoul* (1990), about the then-untitled *V.* The memo-writer informs the recipient, probably Corlies Smith,[10] Pynchon's editor at Lippincott, that Donadio was delighted to hear that the novel would be published and goes on to say that she will get in touch with Pynchon and tell him the news, though there was some question about where he was living. Donadio had "heard nothing [from him] in *months*" but apparently gave Lippincott two addresses at which he might be found: 4754 22d St., N.E., Seattle 5 and 4709½ 9th St., N.E., Seattle.[11]

Pynchon, it would seem, moved to the second address between Donadio's last contact with him and when he sent her the typescript, which was delivered to Lippincott via Donadio's office. The second address may have been the return address on the package Donadio had received, probably in early June and apparently without a small personal note.[12] Because of the lack of contact between the two, Donadio appears to have been uncertain if she had Pynchon's address or someone else's and perhaps thought that he was using the new one to pick up mail, as he had likely done with the two addresses at which Smith wrote to Pynchon prior to August 1961. That, in any case, must have been the thinking at Lippincott, for the memo-writer notes, before passing on the addresses, "Gave me what seems to be a firm address."[13] Those at Lippincott remained uncertain: the memo states that any correspondence should be sent to both addresses, with original material going to the first and copies to the second.

More interesting, given what we know about the transformation of the untitled typescript Lippincott received into *V.*, is that Lippincott was willing to publish the book virtually unchanged, having told Donadio that "any suggestions we would have would probably be in the form of questions, and stressed that our enthusiasm would not be tempered in the least if he chose neither to answer nor make changes in response to those questions." This latter remark suggests that Pynchon had acquired a reputation at Lippincott for being unwilling to discuss his work—likely because he would say nothing, not even to Donadio, according to Smith (Tomaske, May 10, 2001), about the novel when Lippincott signed the contract with him in January 1960 and would also not discuss it when he met Smith in Seattle later in 1960[14]—and thus wouldn't be willing to suffer through the usual exchange between writer and editor. The inability to pin down an exact address at which to write Pynchon must certainly have added to Lippincott's impression of him, hence the wariness about approaching him about making changes to his work. Indeed, friends sensed a circumspection in him, even privately. "Pynchon himself," for instance, "almost never talked about his parents, especially in his earlier years" (48), Boris Kachka, drawing on Tharaldsen's memories, notes.[15]

The lack of data to corroborate is what those such as Lane believe gives them the liberty to spin tales, acknowledge the likelihood of their fictitiousness, and then build upon them as if they were plausible, creating, in effect, the Tom/Thomas division. That division is again brought to the fore in *Bleeding Edge*'s promotional t-shirts—the one in the book trailer and the one handed out to people—apparently to satirize Pynchon's own attempts to remove "Tom," or the idea of him, from the public sphere altogether. Those wearing the shirts are obviously not Pynchon, but only one shirt, the one that Sleazus wears, has the informal "Tom" on it, perhaps drawing attention to the fictional quality of even the private figure as perceived by the public, especially because the character wearing the shirt bears absolutely no resemblance to the person the public imagines Pynchon to be.[16] A version of the character more aligned to the public's perception of him could have left audiences wondering if the video served as some sort of self-revelation. Indeed, the German book trailer, with its trench-coated, elderly—that is, more realistic—Pynchon character, whose face is either kept out of the video-frame or blurred as he wanders through the office building of the German publisher Rowohlt, simultaneously gestures toward the idea that the video is a site of authorial revelation and undermines it through its use of references to the fiction, one of which appears on a t-shirt, perhaps an allusion to the use of t-shirts in the U.S. promotional campaign. The Pynchon character makes other such references in his narration, and the building itself, which is described as "a labyrinth, almost like my novels," is absorbed into the fiction: its temperature, or at least that of one of its offices—3° Celsius or 37° Fahrenheit, "a sign of the apocalypse"—is the same as that of Washington, DC, in the short story "Entropy" (1961). The video possesses "the exact degree of fictitiousness [derived from Pynchon's own pen] to permit" (*AtD* 36) it to display a realistic representation of the author.

Who Pynchon is could be, as far as we can really know, far different from anything we have imagined. He is often called a recluse, a word that is almost invariably used to describe him in newspaper and magazine articles, despite his discounting the label when he was drawn into speaking with CNN, in 1997, after the network caught him on film and threatened to point out who he was on the air: "My belief," he said, "is that 'recluse' is a code word generated by journalists . . . meaning, 'doesn't like to talk to reporters.'"[17] Who, we might ask, is the recluse? Certainly not Tom: some of those belonging to his circle of friends are well known; he was "rarely without a girlfriend for the 30 years" (Kachka 46) before he got married; and he has lived with his wife for more than 25 years and with their son for at least 18 of those. Reclusiveness is a quality publicly attributed to Pynchon, not embraced by him.[18] The recluse of Pynchon's story is not Tom but Thomas Pynchon, the public figure and the name on the promotional-campaign t-shirts that were worn by a number of different people, whom we presumably are to see as his fans and whose ideas about him could be as varied as their faces.

Bleeding Edge's publicity campaign, then, can be said to be, in part, about the public effect of the strategies Pynchon employs to ensure his privacy, adding an extra level of relevance to its promotional value in that both the video and the novel serve as meta-commentaries to the aspect of Pynchon's career in which they participate. The novel at at least one point turns to a consideration of Pynchon's own fiction, specifically *V.*, reworking what Pynchon likely now regards as a flaw. In his first novel, Pynchon had drawn on Leonard Bernstein's *West Side Story* (1957) to portray New York,[19] an approach to establishing an accurate view of the city comparable to his using in "The Small Rain" (1959) a "uniform service accent" as a Southern accent and failing to realize that "people spoke in a wide number of quite different accents" throughout the South (*SL* 4). *Bleeding Edge* offers a correction to the earlier novel's use of Bernstein's work, imagining a musical of his set in New York's Upper West Side—"not *West Side Story*, the other one" (55)—that tells the story of the neighborhood from a different perspective. It features Robert Moses, the urban planner called, in New York, the "master builder" (Gratz 132), singing,

> Throw those Puerto
> Ricans out in the
> Street—It's just a
> Slum, Tear it all
> d-o-o-own! (55–56).

The New York of *West Side Story*, as well as the elements of *V.* that drew upon it, was one that the city had rejected and that had been translated into a more acceptable form for the sake of the musical and, later, the movie, the power of which is also critiqued in the novel. When they adapted the stage show for the movie (1961)—expanding the influence of its representation—"They even had the chutzpah to actually film [. . .] in the same neighborhood they were destroying" (56), that is, while the city was uprooting "7000 *boricua* families" (55) to make way for Lincoln Center.

If Pynchon has been telling his life story all along, as he told Donadio he was, he has been doing it mostly through his fiction, so such indirectly autobiographical moments as *Bleeding Edge*'s discussion of *West Side Story*, the significance of which to the book and its author is highlighted by the fact that Sleazus sings the imaginary Robert Moses song in the book trailer, take on greater importance to the biographer. One of the best-known examples of Pynchon's splicing autobiographical elements into the fiction is his basing the history of William Slothrop, Tyrone Slothrop's ancestor in *Gravity's Rainbow*, on the history of William Pynchon so that Slothrop's family history parallels Pynchon's own. Less obvious is the perhaps "autobiographical lament" (71), as Luc Herman and Steven Weisenburger call it, in the lines from an untitled song in *Gravity's Rainbow*: "Sometimes I wanna go back north to Humboldt County / Sometimes I think I'll go back East to see my kin" (740), a song that also seems to allude to the pie fight Pynchon is said to have held near his Manhattan Beach apartment when he was writing *Gravity's Rainbow*.

Autobiographical details are present elsewhere in the fiction but are integrated into it in subtle, nearly imperceptible, ways. Andrew Gordon calls attention to one of the ways, as well as to the difficulty of perceiving what those details reveal. Paraphrasing a woman he knew while he was in graduate school who later described herself as an ex-lover of Pynchon, Gordon observes that Pynchon's friends, including the woman, would appear in the novel—*Gravity's Rainbow*, one assumes—that "he was working on" in the mid-sixties. Gordon goes on to write, "If there is ever a biography of Pynchon, someone should investigate that angle," but then remarks, "I once combed through *Gravity*, searching for the character who is supposed to be her; there are just too many, and I couldn't be sure" (171). If someone who knew one of the people who allegedly appear in the novel is unable to determine which character corresponds to the woman he knew,[20] how is a biographer, years after the book was published, to identify the people the characters are based on, beyond repeating Siegel's revelation that "Bianca is based on Chrissie [Wexler, or Jolly]" (*Lineland* 101)? Still, Gordon is correct to ask biographers to become attuned to the autobiographical aspects of the fictional oeuvre. The fiction is as integral to the Pynchon narrative to which biographers are trying to give shape as any of the other data they come across, and Pynchon has admitted to "[d]isplacing [his] personal experience off into other environments" (*SL* 21) in his fiction, as he perhaps does in the following passage from *Gravity's Rainbow*:

> It's the street before your childhood home: stony, rutted and cracked, water shining in puddles. You set out to the left. (Usually in these dreams of home you prefer the landscape to the right—broad night-lawns, towered over by ancient walnut trees, a hill, a wooden fence, hollow-eyed horses in a field, a cemetery.... Your task, in these dreams, is often to cross—under the trees, through the shadows—before something happens. Often you go into the fallow field just below the graveyard, full of autumn brambles and rabbits, where the gypsies live. Sometimes you fly. But you can never rise above a certain height [...]). (*GR* 137)

The neighborhood here is reminiscent of the one in which Pynchon's childhood home at 83 Walnut Avenue was located. Today, there are no broad lawns nearby the street—the name of which, I assume, has something to do with walnut trees—nor are there any fields where horses could be kept, but to the right of Walnut Avenue on the other side of Jericho Oyster Bay Road, the road Walnut Avenue feeds into, there is a street called Farm Hill Lane. The lay of the land surrounding it in 1950 suggests it could very well have been a small farm, perhaps one with horses. Indeed, before the development of the area, horses could have been kept in a number of fields between the street the Pynchons lived on and Farm Hill Lane. Whether there were horses or not, broad lawns were present directly across from the entrance to Walnut Avenue when Pynchon was growing up. One also once found a cemetery, the Wesley United Methodist Church Cemetery, which the most recent Nassau County maps suggests has been removed—despite Google Maps' locating it there still—and a wood occupied the landscape behind it (https://lrv.nassaucountyny.gov/map/?s=25&b=56&l=35).

The correspondence between the layout of the dreamscape and the landscape of Pynchon's childhood neighborhood suggests Pynchon, at least on some level, had his own memories, his own dreams, in mind while writing the passage. The connection doesn't easily lend itself to further exploration. The dreamer is Edward Pointsman, the British Pavlovian, so the neighborhood would be in England, something that doesn't make precise biographical sense. Walnut trees are not native to the British Isles, and those growing there would not, presumably, be ancient. The dream would provide more interpretive meat, at least for those trying to establish autobiographical correspondences, if Slothrop, a character associated with Mingeborough, MA, a stand-in for the area that Pynchon grew up in—or even Prentice, he-who-has-others'-dreams-for-them—were the dreamer.

But even if the dream could be connected to a character that seems clearly related to Pynchon's biography, would it alter our understanding of the passage in *Gravity's Rainbow* or tell us something about the man Tom Pynchon. Those dreams that writers feel obliged to sell—an obligation that Pynchon describes in his introduction to *The Teachings of Don B.* (1992) as one of "several humiliating features about writing fiction" (xvi)—don't get or can't be put into words that are capable of duplicating the originals: "So it's a safe bet that most writers' dreams, maybe even including the best ones, manage to stay untranslated and private after all" (xvi). They are like the picture of Roland Barthes's mother, the Winter Garden Photograph, that is described but not included in *Camera Lucida* (1980). Barthes observes of the picture, "I cannot reproduce [it]. It exists only for me. For you, it would be nothing but an indifferent picture, one of the thousand manifestations of the 'ordinary'; [...] at most it would interest your *studium*: period, clothes, photogeny" (73).

For Barthes, to show the photograph, the one that contains "the truth of the face that I had loved" (67), would be to remove it from its position within his "'private life,' [which] is nothing but that zone of space, of time, where I am not an image, an object" (15), and subject it to what Pynchon calls the "indignity of being observ'd" (*M&D* 707) or subject it to being situated within the *studium*—that is, to being experienced culturally—thereby reifying it. For Pynchon, the humiliation of having to sell one's dreams—to commodify one's privacy—seems to be tied to the writer's need to allow them,[21] if we may play on the etymology of "humiliate," to be grounded, or brought low, as opposed to leaving them emanations of being.[22] The very issue that leaves the writer's dreams untranslated also leaves his privacy intact, perhaps saving the writer from disclosing too much of himself but serving as a humiliation nonetheless. Hence Pynchon calls attention to the problem of the writer's feeling obliged to sell his dreams and the impossibility of the reader fully grasping the truth that those dreams reveal. The lack of correspondence between public description and private experience, Pynchon suggests, undercuts the uses to which biographers are in the habit of putting fiction.[23] Thus, discussing the presence of parallels between Fariña's characters in his novel and the people Fariña knew at Cornell, Pynchon observes, "There isn't much point Naming Names" (xii), employing a diction taken from the era of the Hollywood blacklist that suggests doing so would be a betrayal as well as a fruitless exercise.

"A Dual Man [and Oeuvre], Aimed Two Ways at Once": The Two Directions of Pynchon's Life and Thought

WHEN Pynchon—apparently responding to a comment about the possibility of his writing something autobiographical—told Donadio that he had been telling his life story throughout his career, he added, "Nobody ever wants to listen for some strange reason" (Gussow). His bibliography at the time contained mostly fiction, the short stories and the first three novels. His published nonfiction was limited to his Watts article and the short piece on Oakley Hall's *Warlock* (1958), that is, if we discount the high-school publications, the articles he wrote for Boeing, a couple of letters to the editor, and some occasional writings that saw print even though they weren't expressly written for publication. The introductions with autobiographical musings were to come later, so hearing the life story had been, and continues to be, a complicated endeavor. Pynchon nonetheless remained annoyed by that which was misheard. He, for example, wrote Anthony Burgess after Burgess claimed in a 1973 *Paris Review* interview, "Probably (as Thomas Pynchon never went to Valletta or Kafka to America) it's best to imagine your own foreign country." The short letter to Burgess, which reveals that Pynchon had likely learned of the comment secondhand, questions the validity of making such a claim. "You state, 'Pynchon gives us Malta without having been there.' How do you know this?" (quoted in Foster). Still, one is tempted to make biographical conjectures, accepting "that, 'classicism' aside," as Kachka writes, "all of [Pynchon's] books are in some way autobiographical" (157). The problem with accepting such a statement at face value is that one would get drawn into attempting to make the "autobiographical context," as David Foster Wallace calls it in his review of Edwin Williamson's *Borges: A Life* (2004), explain the work.

Kachka himself indulges in such a maneuver. Helping to build a narrative that casts *Bleeding Edge* as Pynchon's return to New York,[24] he calls Horst, who is engaged in a sort of homecoming, the novel's "Pynchon stand-in." Horst, after all, "confesses at Ikea that his 'ideal living space is a not too ratty motel room in the deep Midwest, somewhere up in the badlands' [298]" (158), a supposed allusion to Pynchon's life in the seventies and eighties when he led, it is commonly assumed, a peripatetic existence. Horst also spends perhaps too much time inside watching television, something that reflects, the evidence suggests, a habit Pynchon has or had. The equation, nonetheless, is too straightforward. If we are looking for stand-ins for the author in *Bleeding Edge*, Maxine, whose home has always been New York, serves our purpose as much as Horst, something demonstrated by her "conscious effort not to go near" (51) Times Square since it was cleaned up, a protest against what I call in my review of the novel "the connection between commercialization and the flattening of life's choices" (Rolls 2013). Pynchon had recognized such a connection decades earlier, complaining in a letter from Seattle to Kirkpatrick Sale, for example, that "little old ladies on relief have been evicted to make way for tourists" coming to town for the Seattle World's Fair, which Pynchon described as an excuse for retailers to raise prices. He thus promised to boycott the Fair, going on to worry, in terms Maxine echoes to express her nostalgia for the old Times Square, that if Seattle's city planners get their way, "Skid Road will go, the winos will be made to shave and join AA, they'll turn Pioneer Square into a parking lot" (May 28, 1962).

Pynchon's self-presentation through *Bleeding Edge*'s characters, if we accept that Horst and Maxine share identifying characteristics with their creator, illustrates a double sidedness to his understanding of his own character, as if Pynchon saw himself, as does Fausto of *V.*'s "Generation of '37"—the year of Pynchon's birth and the apocalyptic temperature of the story "Entropy"[25]—as "a dual man, aimed two ways at once: toward peace and simplicity on the one hand, towards an exhausted intellectual searching on the other" (309). From the very beginning of his career, such duality has been a feature of Pynchon's use of authorial stand-ins. The main characters of *V.*'s two plotlines are capable of being read as such. Profane could be categorized as a Pynchon figure because Pynchon, at least if reports are accurate, slept in Kirkpatrick Sale's "spare tub" (Nichols 68)[26] just as Profane sleeps in Kook's family's tub (see 36), and because both did stints in the navy as well as road work (see Siegel 86). We could, however, just as easily develop a correspondence between Pynchon and Stencil, if only because Pynchon loosely appropriated that character's biography for himself,[27] telling Earl Ganz in another documented instance of his fashioning fake autobiographies that his father "was a diplomat [...] had something to do with intelligence," that his childhood reading included top-secret dossiers, and that he had—a little late for Stencil's childhood but still—lived in London in the latter years of the war and remembered "[t]he buzz bombs" (Ganz 13). Pynchon, at least conceptually, identifies himself as inhabiting both of what Lee Konstantinou calls "Stencil's and Profane's irreconcilable positions" (91), those of the quester or postwar modernist and of the anti-quester or post-Beat hipster (see Konstantinou 55 and 90). We might identify other characters who can be associated with Pynchon in similar ways, possibly even Oedipa and Mucho,[28] even though "[s]ome people guarantee that Tharaldsen served as the inspiration for Oedipa" (Portinari), but by the time we get to Maxine and Horst, Maxine—a post-Reagan version of *Inherent Vice*'s Doc Sportello—has taken, as did Doc before her, the position of a hipster-like figure who is also a quester, and Horst, a sort of anti-quester, seems to be in the process of reconciling himself to the quester, that is, Maxine, whom he failed to hold onto earlier in his life.

Trying to determine in unambiguous terms which character might be an authorial stand-in from novel to novel is not necessarily a simple or worthwhile exercise. That is not to say that Pynchon's novels lack characters who serve as figurations of the author in some respect; it is to say that while the stand-ins may attest to the autobiographical character of the oeuvre—which, it can be said, offers material for an implied biography, the very biography Pynchon told Donadio readers would be able to discern if they would only "listen" carefully enough—those stand-ins are, at best, suggestive elements of the life story. Attuning oneself to the autobiographical resonances in Pynchon's fiction is not to expect biography to provide an interpretive grid that can be positioned over the work so that its meaning can be explained, nor should we expect to be able to "use the work to interpret the life" (111), which Susan Sontag, drawing on Walter Benjamin, suggests would be a better approach. Rather, the work and the biography should together provide the material with which the critic–biographer builds the text s/he is writing so that background and foreground don't simply reflect each other but are shown to meet at certain points of convergence, *puncta* we might call them, appropriating Barthes's term. Some of these points may involve characters and the people, including the author, whom they are modeled after; other points, ones that are less clearly autobiographical but are perhaps more interesting, can be just as revealing, if not more so.

I

The introduction of the name "Denis" in *Inherent Vice*, along with the story about Denis's stop at a local drugstore, is one of those points. The name, because of the pronunciation, and drugstore tale are, at least when first encountered, groan inducing, the verbal equivalent of the child's bad teeth that Barthes stubbornly sees (45) in William Klein's photograph "Little Italy, New York" (1954). Hence James Parker begins his review with the quip, "If Thomas Pynchon were a stand-up comedian, and *Inherent Vice* his newest routine, the heckling would start around page 10. 'So Doc,' relates a character called Denis (whose name, we are informed, is commonly pronounced to rhyme with—heh, heh—'penis'), 'I'm up on Dunecrest, you know the drugstore there, and like I noticed their sign, "Drug"? "Store"? Okay? Walked past it a thousand times, never *really saw it*—Drug, Store! man, far out, so I went in and Smilin Steve was at the counter and I said, like, "Yes, hi, I'd like some drugs, please...."'" The forced play on the name and the too easily arrived at drug pun both strike the reader as sophomoric, while the pun seems clichéd, further below Pynchon's intelligence than we would like to think he would stoop. To discount them and move on, or throw the book across the room as Parker half implies we should do, however, would be to lose sight of "that high magic to low puns" (*CL49* 129), not only blinding ourselves to the sensibility of a man who staged a pie fight near his apartment and who, his friend Phyllis Gebauer recalled, enjoys the corniest of humor[29] but also preventing us from appreciating the ingenuity of *Inherent Vice* and, ultimately, Pynchon's take on the Sixties and what followed it. The fictional moment, like each "*punctum*[,] has, more or less potentially, a power of expansion," an expansion, in the present case, into the fiction and, from there, the life. "This power is [...] metonymic" (Barthes 45).

Denis's name and the play on the idea of the drugstore unite two parts of what is sometimes, both within the novel and elsewhere, accepted as a strict binary division between the straight world and drug culture,[30] capturing a recurring concern of *Inherent Vice*, the question of which side one is on—an issue that *Vineland* (1990) also addresses and that Coy Harlingen raises more openly in Paul Thomas Anderson's 2014 filmic adaptation of the novel[31]—and establishing one of the more subtle elements of the novel's textual environment. The pun on "drugs," in a somewhat obvious way, calls attention to and undermines the division between substances that contribute to the formation of the freak community and those prescribed by doctors, as does Lieutenant Pat Dubonnet's disappointment with a career reduced to "penny-ante collars, kids under the pier dealing their moms' downers" (47). Indeed, the name of the drugstore employee whom Denis asks for drugs, Smilin Steve, as well as Denis's and Doc's familiarity with him, marks him as someone more likely to be connected with a place like Tommy's, where for an extra fifty cents one could get a joint wrapped in wax paper in one's "cheezburger" (73).[32] The breakdown of the division, at least between the licit and the illicit use of drugs, is also worked into and undermined within Doc's professional environment apropos of Dr. Buddy Tubeside's "B_{12}" clinic, from which the doctor, in order to keep things flowing smoothly in the so-called straight world, distributes amphetamines to a collection of melancholy housewives, actors looking for work, professional schmoozers, and tired stewardii, along with the occasional legitimate B_{12}-deprived cases who presumably get the vitamin.

That Tubeside is distributing amphetamines complicates the issue. That drug, along with downers, is associated more with members of the criminal underworld than hippies, a distinction the straight world isn't inclined to acknowledge.

Doc feels obliged to explain to Lieutenant "Bigfoot" Bjornsen, for instance, that Glen Charlock and his associates have "totally the wrong drug profile, too many reds, too much speed" (26), for Doc to be counted as one of them. Bigfoot ignores the lesson, insisting on including Doc in the same category as Glen when he remarks in malicious jest that Glen's murderer might "turn out to be one of those perpetrators who *specially like* to murder hippies" (29). This complication adds to the sense that the simple equation of drug use with the counterculture is losing its significance or has always been imprecise. Just as the distinction between hippies and Nazi bikers has no significance—because both groups are associated with drugs—for those charged with maintaining the straight world's order, the distinction between "flatland" culture and hippie culture is not necessarily one that needs to be acknowledged. Drugs pervade both of them.

The play on the name "Denis" gestures toward the same issue, demonstrating the novel's use of what might be dubbed learned low humor. Whether it rhymes with "penis" or not, the name is English for the Greek "Dionysios" or the Latin "Dionysius" and is "from the Greek, [follower of or] 'belonging to the god of wine'" (*Standard Dictionary of Facts* 811). Pynchon's pronunciation joke, at the very least, calls attention to the pre-Christian significance of the name, alluding to the phallic element of the Dionysian cult and perhaps also to Phales, "the personified phallus" (6), as Lowell Edmunds describes that particular companion of Dionysus, whose name also serves as a partial homonym of the name of the male sexual organ. Doc, whom Denis follows when he is needed, can thus be seen in the role of Dionysus, an element of Pynchon's characterization of him to which we will return. In the Christian era, however, the name Dionysius is associated with Dionysius the Areopagite, the Athenian judge whom St. Paul converted (Acts 17:34) and who took on importance to Christian theology after an anonymous sixth-century author—the Pseudo-Dionysius—attributed his own work to Dionysius. The minor Biblical figure thereafter came to be associated with a major strain of medieval theology, particularly the establishment of the most influential vision of the angelic hierarchies (see Arthur). He is, in short, not simply a figure associated with the established order but one who is counted among its architects.

Denis's name therefore points to both a Dionysian register and an Apollonian register, making Denis, metaphorically speaking, a site of Sixties' conflict, much as a drunken Jack Kerouac made himself one, no doubt obliviously, during an appearance on William Buckley's *Firing Line* in 1968. Kerouac observed of the hippie movement—while discussing the relationship between the Beats and the hippies and the part he played in influencing the latter—"apparently it's some kind of Dionysian movement in late civilization, and which I did not intend any more than I suppose Dionysius did, or whatever his name was." Kerouac went on to say, "Although I'm not Dionysius the Areopagite, I should have been," befuddling Buckley, perhaps with good reason. From the context, it is unclear whether Kerouac is confusing the Christian figure with a Greek follower of the wine god or playing off Buckley's description of him as one who "fought his way out of the Beat generation and is now thought exactly orthodox," a characterization Kerouac offers support for when he gives a thumbs down at the mention of Allen Ginsberg, who was in the audience; when he belittles leftists or communists, Lawrence Ferlinghetti in particular, placing them in an associative chain that includes "hoodlums"—just as Bigfoot lumps hippies in with Nazi bikers—all of whom Kerouac complains jumped on his back, in the sense of standing on the shoulders of one's predecessors and/or of burdening him with the weight of their expectations; and when he reveals that he, as well as his family, had always voted Republican (Buckley).[33]

Denis, it is true, seems to represent a pure Dionysian figure, and not simply because of his drug use. Intoxication, after all, is only one aspect of the Dionysian spirit. Denis, like those imbued with that spirit, "feels himself not only united, reconciled, and fused with his neighbor, but as one with him, as if the veil of *māyā* had been torn aside and were now merely fluttering in tatters before the mysterious primordial unity" (Nietzsche 37). The Sixties' manifestation of such a feeling is dissipating—though it may always have been confined to mere moments, and Denis, in any case, isn't prepared to accept the change—in the post-Manson-murder culture of 1970, including among the members of the freak community. The problem, including Denis's lack of awareness, is made particularly evident as Japonica's car passes "Wallach's Music City, where each of a long row of audition booths inside had its own lighted window," behind each of which "appeared a hippie freak or small party of hippie freaks, each listening on headphones to a different rock 'n' roll album and moving around at a different rhythm" (176). The experience of those listeners is contrasted with free outdoor concerts "where thousands of people congregated [. . . and] blended together into a single public self, because everybody was having the same experience" (176).

Denis finds himself within a larger variation of the dissipation of *Vineland*'s PR[3] the night Weed Atman is shot:

> Something was going on up on campus. [. . .] There had been no posters or announcements or indeed anyplace left for communication to come from, only the gathering, in falling dark and confusion without limit, around the fountain in the Plaza where PR[3]ers in their youth had frolicked stoned and nude. Now, with the black rearing silhouette of the Nixon Monument against the sunset, [. . .]

> suddenly no one recognized anyone's face, and each was isolated in a sea of strangers. A common feeling, reported in interviews later, was of a clear break just ahead with everything they'd known. Some said "end," others "transition." (244)

Denis doesn't feel, as the PR³ers do, the contrast between past moments of communal unity and the isolated present, or he willfully ignores it. Intent on digging the moment, he waves, yells, and flashes peace signs in an attempt to forge a connection with each of the booth-dwellers, but he goes unnoticed, a nonreaction to his advances that he tries to disregard with the aid of a pun, the magic of which fails to transform the situation: "Far out. Maybe they're all stoned. Hey! That must be why they call those things *head*phones! [. . .] Think about that, man! Like, *head*phones, right?" (176). Denis's punning on "head" here is an attempt to will his audience to ignore his isolation from the freaks in Wallach's as well as their isolation from each other.[34]

The context undermines that intention: Denis's offering intoxication as an excuse for the booth-dwellers' and his own seclusion undoes the power of the analogy between intoxication and the Dionysian spirit by suggesting that drugs can undermine the sense of community at the heart of hippie culture and generate the *"principium individuationis"* (Nietzsche 36), the principle of Apollo. Denis, in fact, has glorified that principle and demonstrated, if unwittingly, that taking drugs is not necessarily, as Karen M. Staller explains doing so was thought to be in the sixties, "a communal experience that bond[s] the youth community together" (80). Indeed, the assumption that those in the record-store audition booths are stoned marks the freaks as easily recognizable members of a certain demographic. They have become little more than isolated consumers with "no more primary choices [...] to make." They are, as Pynchon writes of his generation's relationship to the Beats, "onlookers: the parade had gone by and [they are] already getting everything secondhand" (*SL* 9), a condition emphasized by the fact that the beats to which each is listening are supplied for the sake of a sale. Their audition for the freak show, to put it another way, is not simply too late but rendered inauthentic by its participation in the commercial simulation of gestures of resistance during those volatile days when "revolution," as *Vineland* puts it, "went blending into commerce" (308).

Hope and Coy Harlingen's plotline partakes of a parallel dynamic, serving as a microcosmic, heroin-inspired variation on the cultural change Denis's experience illustrates. Hope and Coy connect in a toilet stall. Having just smuggled heroin into California from Mexico in balloons they had swallowed, they accidentally come together to discharge their load, Hope with her "finger already down [her] throat, and there Coy sat, gringo digestion, about to take a gigantic shit. [They] both let go at about the same time, barf and shit all over the place [...] and to complicate things of course he had this hardon" (37–38). They had become, to appropriate a formula from a different context, "abjected anarchistic, formless and fluid Dionysian bod[ies]" (Vagelis Siropoulos, cited in Yebra 192); they embody in that moment the abject, as Julia Kristeva defines it, encompassed as they are by excrement and vomit, but not to demarcate the boundaries that separate their selves from that which is other. Rather, they return, metaphorically speaking, to the gap between the period of infancy and the period after a child's subjectivity has developed, a time when the self-other boundary has not yet been fully established, and prepare to fuse, something suggested by the complication raised by Coy's hardon.

His erection demonstrates his lacking a feeling of loathing despite being covered in vomit, which Jacques

"Derrida once, in fact, explicitly privileged [. . .] as the disgustingly unassimilable 'other' of the beautiful and the moral, serving philosophy therefore as 'an elixir, even in the very quintessence of bad taste'" (Jay 239). Coy thus signals his desire "to reintegrate [with his other half] [. . .], to make two into one, and to bridge the gulf between one human being and another," which is love's function as Plato's Aristophanes explains it in the *Symposium* (191d) when he tells the myth of the Androgynes, those creatures in whom lovers, man and woman as well as same-sex combinations, were originally unified (191d–e).

Hope and Coy's subsequent marriage, "less than two weeks later" (39), supplements—with all the ambiguity Derrida brings to that term—the moment in which they met. Marrying "on the interesting theory that two can score as cheaply as one" (39), they follow a drug inspired variation of the biblical notion that "the two shall become one flesh" (Matthew 19:5), transforming the spirituality of marriage into a reiteration of their material achievement in the stall, a site to which their need to score had brought them. Their heroin addiction, however, undermines their oneness, particularly after Amethyst, their daughter, is born, leading them to understand that they were "dragging each other down" and needed to "come up with something" (192) to escape the "cycle," to appropriate Hope's description of middle-class life, "of choices that are no choices at all" (38) that they have become trapped within, a trap Hope links to middle-class life when she makes an analogy between shooting up and drinking cocktails. The trap, in fact, is undermining the health of the period, which was sometimes called the Age of Aquarius, the birthstone of which is now the "swollen, red-faced, vacant" (*IV* 38) Amethyst. Hope and Coy's understanding that their common addiction is a drag on their aspirations, or perhaps on their chance of ever having any aspirations beyond "a world of hassle reduced to the one simple issue of scoring" (38), seems to reveal that a middle-class mindset had always been an element of their sensibilities and had merely been manifesting itself in a form not immediately recognizable as such. Their existence, like Denis's name, points in two directions.

Drugs, at least heroin and amphetamines, are linked in the novel to the same kind of consumption that lulls those in the middle class into their contentment and also to an inability to find or sustain the type of unity Coy and Hope—who "should've met cute" (37), as *Nineteen-Eighty Four*'s Winston and Julia do (see Pynchon's Foreword xxii)[35]—stumble upon in the bathroom stall. Certain drugs are presented as analogues of television, the new opium of the people, an idea familiar from Dr. Deeply's tubaldetox organization, the "National Endowment for Video Education and Rehabilitation" (NEVER), in *Vineland* (33). In *Inherent Vice*, the commonalities between drugs and television are hinted at with regard to amphetamines in Dr. Tubeside's name and are more pointedly brought to the fore when Denis sets up, as if it were a television, the twenty kilos of heroin Doc has hidden in a box that originally contained a twenty-five-inch color TV: "And dig it, Doc, if you watch long enough . . . see how it begins to sort of . . . change?" (339). Doc and, soon after, Jade/Ashley acquiesce to the observation, and they all—Denis, Doc, and Jade/Ashley—gather like "some wholesome family [. . .] to gaze tubeward," or, I guess, heroinward, and gobble their snacks, just as Bigfoot imagines some family doing "on a future homesite" in Channel View Estates (22).

Inherent Vice is no simple piece of nostalgia, as some critics complained upon its release. It is an examination of the consumerist tendencies that link members of the Sixties' counterculture to mainstream culture and Pynchon's response to that problem. By the mid-seventies at the latest, Pynchon recognized, and apparently felt distraught over, what was happening, seeing that the way things were developing was undermining the power of the period's social movements. In a 1974 letter to David Shetzline and Mary (M. F.) Beal, Pynchon discusses an upcoming rally for the impeachment of Richard Nixon, satirizing its purpose by suggesting that it will be more of a social event for the fashionably leftist than a politically engaged expression of outrage: "Maybe I am wrong not to show up, after all think of all that great neurotic pussy that always shows up at things like—oh, aww, gee Mary, I'm sorry! I meant 'vagina,' of course!—like that, and all the biggies who'll be there." Correcting himself by writing that he meant "vagina" does not change the tenor of the comment, but Pynchon is doing something other than being boorish, even though in the two places where the joke turns up in the fiction (see *Vl* 73 and *AtD* 438), substituting "vagina" for "pussy" serves as a superficial correction meant to appease a listener's sensibility rather than to illustrate an alteration in the speaker's thinking. Pynchon likely wasn't expecting Shetzline and Beal to believe he would go to the rally to pick up a woman he had never met. Those who know Pynchon don't regard him as a man prone to such behavior. As Tharaldsen, who lived with him in the mid-sixties, told Kachka, "He was very withdrawn, and the one way he could make connections with women would be through his friends" (153).[36]

The letter projects the superficiality displayed by Pynchon's fictional characters who utter the joke onto those who will be attending the rally, among whom Pynchon was not to be counted. Replacing the offensive "pussy" with the PC "vagina" is analogous to exchanging the nightclub scene for the political-rally scene, because the protest's value lies in its creating an opportunity for people to pick each other up and see celebrities, who will be there not merely to protest but also to be seen, or consumed. Pynchon associates the type of cultural consumption that will be on display with lateness, that is, the secondhand reception and simulation of gestures and attitudes associated with those who developed them: he thus asks in the letter, "Why didn't they have one [an anti-Nixon rally] in '68?"

Hippies, Pynchon suggests, were—perhaps were always already—in the process of being absorbed into the world they opposed, becoming just another subset of the larger community, not necessarily as Shasta Fay seems to have become, "all in flatland gear [...] looking just like she swore she'd never look" (1), but in hippie gear, a uniform that identifies the market to which they belong. They might wear the clothes, listen to the music, take the drugs, and attend the political rallies, but they do so in a spirit that subverts the hope hippie culture represented for those of a certain disposition, apparently including Pynchon. They are, as Brock Vond cynically puts it in *Vineland*, "amateurs, consumers, short attention spans, out there for the thrills, pick up a chick, score some dope, nothing political" (270). Vond's characterization of those who make up the counterculture, ninety percent of its members by his estimate, seems to be confirmed by the name "PR^3." The name implies that the PR^3 protesters—in contrast to *V.*'s McClintic Sphere, whose "name was chosen because a sphere is a non-square in 3 dimensions" (To Faith Sale, November 23, 1962)[37]—are, despite superficial appearances, square, or cubed, which we would realize if we could see them as three-dimensional characters rather than unrecognizable faces on the scene. "Movement coordinators" thus find them to be kids who hadn't "been doing any analysis. Not only was nobody thinking about the real situation, nobody was even brainlessly reacting to it. Instead they were busy surrounding [themselves] with a classically retrograde cult of personality" (205) developed around Weed Atman. Such "politically disguised hero worship engenders fascism" (205), as Robert R. Hill observes, or, perhaps it would be more correct to say, is rooted in the same impulse that fascism is rooted in. That the PR³ers' spontaneous revolt is maintained as a community by means of a fascist impulse points to their inability to commit to revolutionary ideals or their republic's inability to serve as a nostalgic representation of a "serious 1960s model of social reciprocity" (202), as Hill maintains it does, despite his noting that Pynchon understands it is flawed. They don't put in, to cite Sphere, "the slow, frustrating and hard work" (*V.* 365) needed to escape, as Joanna Freer writes in another context, the "negative choice between simple acquiescence in the victory of the oppressors and all-out war" (70).[38]

The ostensible communal cohesion of the PR³, because it is developed without analysis, does not represent in Pynchon's oeuvre some model for which we should strive. It is more like the media-generated national cohesion that authorities in *Bleeding Edge* attempt to forge (with the aid of PR, we might say) in the aftermath of 9/11, an event that provides a rallying cause around which national consensus can be justified and embraced or enforced. The official narrative (almost like an actual charismatic leader) that emerges in the novel's post-9/11 atmosphere offers the population the idea that it is safely ensconced "inside some extended national Family" (*Vl* 269), to appropriate Vond's notion about the deeper meaning of the majority of hippies' behavior. That narrative infuses traces of its perspective into the language that we become obliged to use to talk about what happened. Take, for example, "Ground Zero," the name given to the site of the collapsed Twin Towers. It is "a Cold War term taken from the scenarios of nuclear war so popular in the early sixties. This was nowhere near a Soviet nuclear strike on downtown Manhattan, yet those who repeat 'Ground Zero' over and over do so without shame or concern for etymology. The purpose is to get people cranked up in a certain way. Cranked up, scared, and helpless" (328). It doesn't matter, from a certain perspective, if some, to return to Vond's formulation, are "listening to the wrong music, breathing the wrong smoke, admiring the wrong personalities" (*Vl* 269), that is, it doesn't matter if they are attending to or serving as oppositional voices—which in *Bleeding Edge* are represented by those developing a "different [darker] picture [. . .] in the vast undefined anarchism of cyberspace" (*BE* 327)—so long as what they speak echoes the voice of officialdom each time, in the example from *Bleeding Edge*, they name the site where the atrocity took place. It is something like Mucho's perception that "[e]verybody who says the same words is the same person if the spectra are the same only they happen differently in time, you dig? But the time is arbitrary" (*CL49* 142). "Same person," in the context of *Bleeding Edge*, becomes "representative of authorized thought."

Ground Zero, as I have argued elsewhere, thereby enters a commercial environment, coming to serve as "a product, the brand name of which has been genericized without having to compete with an alternative brand, and the press, 'the Newspaper of Record' (388) in particular," coming to serve as "just a medium through which to conduct the advertising campaign" (Rolls 2013). Such commercialization manifests itself in a different form in Pynchon's representation of the unwinding of the Sixties but generates the same effect, undermining the power of dissidence, the language of which is coopted for the purpose of connecting it to what it opposes. This element of Pynchon's thinking is made clear when Bigfoot appears in the commercials for Channel View Estates wearing an "ankle-length velvet cape in paisley print of so many jangling 'psychedelic' hues" (*IV* 9), a look Paul Thomas Anderson, according to the script (9), sought to duplicate on film. Anderson also planned to use children—who are portrayed in the novel as using phrases associated with hippies—but opted for having Bigfoot alone in a large oval on the television screen. Bigfoot's diction mimics that of the counterculture—as it includes "hey man," "pad," "grooviest," "buzz kill," "rip off," "check this out," "out of sight," and "right on"—while he touts the value of the future homes. Images of a middle-class housing development and the Dominguez flood-control channel flash in the background. Anderson's changes may capture the implications of the novel's commercial better than a closer duplication of Pynchon's vague description of the particular ad would have. Pynchon is able to depict Bigfoot's work in the series of Channel-View-Estates commercials, whereas Anderson is obliged to focus on one. Anderson's juxtaposition of the hippie-looking spokesman with stills of middle-class life suggests the counterculture can be incorporated into the American Dream, just as the idea of a hippie-looking spokesman's appearance in a repetitive series normalizes his presence.[39]

Housing estates can channel, to play on the name Pynchon gives Mickey Wolfmann's project, the flood of dissidents if such people can be led to perceive embracing the American Dream in terms compatible with their idiomatic attitudes. The cost of their accepting the pitch and taking the mortgage that, according to the movie, will accompany the no-money-down offer, and of their holding a straight-world job to pay for it, will undercut their ability to be counter to anything and turn each of them into a representation of what Pynchon calls in his Watts article "the *little* man—meaning not so much any member of the power structure [the Man] as just your average white L.A. taxpayer, registered voter, property owner; employed, stable, mortgaged and the rest" (80). That element of the project is evinced by the fact that Tariq Khalil's neighborhood has been torn down to make way for the development, which Tariq sees as revenge for Watts (17). The thinking about those to be placed in the housing estate is, however, also analogous to the thinking about Watts residents that Pynchon ascribes to the L.A. power structure, now transposed to deal with at least the white elements of the counterculture: "Give them a little property, and they will be less tolerant of arson; get them to go in hock for a car or color TV, and they'll be more likely to hold down a steady job" ("JMW" 84). Wolfmann's plan to give away housing would have helped to counter the ability of "the Man" to turn hippies into "little men" and get them to abandon their tolerance for elements of the countercultural with which they are not necessarily in accord.

II

The Sixties or its values—despite the critique of the ease with which those embracing its ethos became consumers of its features and thereby allowed those in power to commercialize it—remain a positive force in Pynchon's thought. The idealism of the period is recalled by March Kelleher in *Bleeding Edge*; her admiration for certain techies is derived from their spirit, which she hasn't "seen anything like [. . .] since the sixties. These kids are out to change the world. 'Information has to be free'" (116). The association of early twenty-first-century hackers with the Sixties' counterculture links the setting free of information with drugs, just as *Inherent Vice*'s "ARPAnet trip [is] like acid, a whole 'nother strange world" (195), logging-on to which, to use today's terminology, feels "like doing psychedelics" (365) after a while. For Pynchon, the use of drugs, particularly LSD and marijuana—although Takeshi's amphetamine consumption in *Vineland* seems also to be included, suggesting that context as well as the particular substance is important—is, as David Cowart puts it, "a metaphor serving the vision of a different social reality" (98). Even in his nonfiction, Pynchon in 1984 calls marijuana "that useful substance" (*SL* 8), and in his 1992 introduction to *The Teachings of Don B.*, he observes of Texas—displaying his understanding of its landscape, both in the mid-sixties when he lived in Houston and in the present—"The nearest venue for dope, sex, and rock 'n' roll, then as now, was Austin" (xix). That may be a historical mischaracterization but is symbolically accurate if the triad of Sixties' revolution is understood as something other than physical reality; within Texas, Austin represents an alternative world, one removed from the notorious conservative culture that prompts the following exchange in Hunter S. Thompson's "The Great Shark Hunt": "'Are you ready to get busted in Texas? [. . .] Remember Tim Leary? [. . .] Ten years for three ounces of grass in his daughter's panties. . . .' 'Jesus . . . Texas! I'd forgotten about that'" (439).

The Sixties, as we are to understand it, isn't so much the decade as the mythology of the decade, as evidenced in *Inherent Vice* by the figure of Vehi, who can indulge in "systematic daily [acid] tripping" (105), a fantasy of and about acidheads but, given the tolerance to the drug that one immediately builds up, not actually possible.[40] If Pynchon were shooting for realism, he would have written "weekly tripping." The more powerful illustration of this element of Pynchon's thinking is expressed in Zoyd and Mucho's recollection of that "windowpane, down in Laguna." Zoyd begins the exchange with "God, I knew then, I knew. . . ." Mucho continues:

> "Uh-huh, me too. That you were never going to die. Ha! No wonder the state panicked. How are they supposed to control a population that knows it'll never die? When that was always their last big

chip, when they thought they had the power of life and death. But acid gave us the X-ray vision to see through that one, so of course they had to take it away from us." (313–14)

What we have here (as Pynchon describes it in "Is It O.K. to Be a Luddite?") is

> a profound unwillingness to give up elements of faith [or, in the context of Mucho's remarks, to ignore new insights], however 'irrational,' to an emerging technopolitical order that might or might not know what it was doing. [. . .] To insist on the miraculous is to deny to the machine at least some of its claims on us, to assert the limited wish that living things, earthly and otherwise, may on occasion become Bad and Big enough to take part in transcendent doings. (173)

The Sixties, as anthropomorphized metaphor, is the Dionysian body as Badass, not a Ned Lud, the historical figure whose name grew bigger than the man, but "King (or Captain) Ludd" (170), the mythologized character that such growth created. Like other literary Badasses, Pynchon's Sixties is pulled together from fragments, the disparate voices of the counterculture—college kids, surfers, hippies, Afro-American militants, and various leftists (see Freer, particularly 12–13)—and, like other makers of such legendary creatures, Mary Shelley and Horace Walpole in particular, Pynchon's narrator uses "voices not [his] own" ("Luddite" 172), noting of Zoyd and Mucho's exchange, "It was the way people used to talk" (314).

The "used to" registers not just the disconnect between the narrator's voice and that of the Sixties but also the loss of the hope that was present in the voice of the past, thereby suggesting the suppression of the idea that change is possible and raising the question, What can we do to recover what has been lost? Pynchon's letter to Shetzline and Beal, like *Inherent Vice,* is also concerned with this question or, more specifically, with the problem of deciding what to do in the face of what Pynchon calls in *Bleeding Edge* the "stupefied consensus about what life is to be" (51), a consensus that is regaining its strength as "the Psychedelic Sixties, this little parenthesis of light" (*IV* 254), comes to an end. This end is associated in *Inherent Vice* with the movie *He Ran All the Way* (1951), "John Garfield's last picture before the antisubversives finally did him in, and it had the smell of blacklist all over it" (254).[41] In the letter, claiming he is "[h]aving what the CIA calls a 'mid-life crisis,'"—a phrase taken, according to the footnote, from "Ellsberg's dossier," that is, the Pentagon Papers—Pynchon muses about finding "another hustle [...] I cannot dig to live a 'literary' life no more, maybe will try to learn putting cane seats in chairs, something clear and useful like that anyway, shit, you must know what I mean."

Caning seats is comparable in its significance (at least as it is presented in the letter) to finding "a lump of hash," which, Pynchon writes, he had made inquiries about while travelling around the West coast on Greyhound buses in the fall of 1973. "I lost [it] someplace," he continues, "in Humboldt County 3 years ago and am still brooding about [it . . .] yes, SYMBOLIC! all right, that occurred to me too: that lump of hash was my good times all right, besides being real, secular Good Shit." His finding a lump of hash three-years gone and learning a manual skill are not, of course, ideas to be taken at face value. Rather, Pynchon's thinking about them is a symptom of his brooding over an apparent lack of possibilities. They are notions that point toward a past and a possible future that contain value in contrast to a present devoid of any clear purpose beyond that afforded by "aimless drifting," something Pynchon, if what he tells Shetzline and Beal is to be believed, had been pursuing for two years or so. Pynchon suggests he is going to curtail such travel, as he is "keying [his] plans on Geraldine [his then-girlfriend], part of a general resolution not to impose shit on her" by turning his own peripatetic life into an oppressive force.[42]

Pynchon portrays himself as someone caught on a threshold, the one at the exit of the psychedelic parenthesis, itself a liminal period,[43] unable to go back and unsure about how to go forward. The following year he seems to have been feeling better about his profession. He wrote to Donadio to tell her about a novel he was working on that would deal with Mason and Dixon (Gussow), a book he may have been considering writing since as early as 1970, if not before (Kachka 52). This project—as well as another one, a book said to be titled "The Japanese Insurance Adjuster" that was rumored to feature the Japanese movie monster Mothra and that never came to fruition but traces of which seem to be present in *Vineland*[44]—was, it is reasonable to assume, Pynchon's attempt to revive the possibilities of his life as a writer. Writing "was all I was good for" (To Kirkpatrick and Faith Sale, March 27, 1964),[45] he had speculated when he considered giving it up to pursue a bachelor's degree in mathematics in the early sixties. In the early eighties, he continued to feel caught, deploring in an undated letter to Michael Stephens, a member of Columbia University's Writing Program, the state of American publishing for "proving more & more dangerous to my mental health, with these bullshit nickel-and-dimers in control. If there was a budget time-machine service around, I'd hop in, go back 20 years and look around for another hustle,'"[46] echoing a phrase he had used in the Shetzline–Beal letter a decade earlier.

The fiction reflects Pynchon's state of in-betweenness. The apparently Mothra-based elements of *Vineland* involve Takeshi Fumimoto—who is introduced "standing at the edge of a gigantic animal footprint" (142)—during a peripatetic period, when his "one fixed address," now that he is "out on his own," is "a cubicle in outer Ueno he shared rent on" (143). The edge that he is standing on, at least in *Vineland* if not in "The Japanese Insurance Adjuster," is also the edge of a new phase of his life, between his life as an independent investigator of insurance claims for Wawazume Life & Non-Life and his life with DL Chastain, freelancing in the Karmic adjustment business, for example, among the Thanatoids. More striking, *Mason & Dixon* (1997) has a liminal space, the line between the North and the South, at its center, a space that, as the story of the making of the line comes to an end, is imagined as potentially endless:

> Suppose that Mason and Dixon and their Line cross Ohio after all. [. . .] The under-lying Condition of their Lives is quickly establish'd as the Need to keep, as others a permanent address, a perfect Latitude,— no fix'd place, rather a fix'd Motion[. . . .] Whenever they do stop moving [. . .] they lose their Invisibility." (706, 707)

The pursuit of limitless potential, something Pynchon may have sought in his own analogue to the line, *Gravity's Rainbow* (1973)—a project rumored while in progress to be regarded as "an endless novel" (Gordon 171)—must, even if imaginary, be interrupted, and Mason and Dixon's equally imaginary discovery of "the first new Planet" (708), Uranus, fifteen years before the fact, sends them eastward in the hope of settling into a life of material excess, a detail that suggests America's potential got lost in the pursuit of wealth for its own sake.[47]

This return trip is complicated by the extension of the line over the Atlantic and by the itinerant community that comes to form around its "transnoctially charter'd 'Atlantick Company'" (714). The two, now feeling neither "British enough anymore, nor quite American," settle into retirement on this mid-Atlantic line—a doubly liminal space, that is, longitudinally and latitudinally so—"content to reside like Ferrymen or Bridge-keepers, ever in a Ubiquity of Flow, before a ceaseless Spectacle of Transition" (714).[48]

In 1983—after what Pynchon refers to as "this decade of Writer's Block I seem to be having & all"—he was still feeling insecure, he reveals in a letter to Donald Barthelme, about his being a writer, a feeling similar to what he had felt after the publication of *V.* and presumably had grappled with on and off throughout the years. As he had done in his 1974 letter to Shetzline and Beal, Pynchon presents himself to Barthelme as a wanderer, telling him that he remained, Takeshi-like, without a "fixed address" and had been "between coasts, Arkansas or Lubbock or someplace like 'at"[49] on March 17, when the literary dinner to which Barthelme had invited him took place. A year later, in 1984, the sources Helen Dudar drew upon for her *Chicago Tribune Book World* article, "Lifting the Veil on Life of a Literary Recluse," offered accounts that correspond to that self-presentation: "What can be gathered personally about Pynchon from those who have shared his company is that he is a restless, rootless man who lives, as unencumbered as possible, from place to place and coast to coast in borrowed or sublet quarters" (Dudar 35).[50]

The idea of the peripatetic Pynchon, however, was something of an artifice, even if Pynchon himself had fashioned it. He was living at the Sales' New York City apartment in the year before *Gravity's Rainbow* appeared, well within the two-year period during which he told Shetzline and Beal he had been drifting, and in the years before his writing to Barthelme he must have spent considerable time in New York, possibly settling there after returning from England, where he travelled around 1978, and staying a long enough time to establish a close relationship with Melanie Jackson in the lead-up to his break with Donadio and with much of his past.[51] Barthelme, in any case, thought Pynchon was there, even though Pynchon seems to have been keeping his distance from those he had spent time with in the early seventies. He feels the need to draw Barthelme's attention to his change of agents—a change that took place at the beginning of 1982, although the event that caused it took place in 1981,[52] more than a year before his receiving the invitation—and notes that he may have seen Barthelme "on the street once last year or maybe the year before, in the Village, but [. . .] failed to say hello." Pynchon's aimlessness seems to have manifested itself more as mental wandering than in physical action, even if he turned to the road from time to time.

The predicament of the characters in *Inherent Vice* is in some respects the one Pynchon seems to have faced for an extended period after the publication of *Gravity's Rainbow*, that is, dealing with the loss of hope that the social movements of the Sixties had unleashed. Pynchon seems to have filled the void, in part, by watching T.V. In the mid-seventies, when Judith Pynchon was asked what her brother might be doing at the moment, she replied, "Probably watching *The Brady Bunch*. It's his favorite show." *Vineland* may thus come off, as it did to David Foster Wallace, as if Pynchon had "spent 20 years smoking pot and watching T.V." (Max 152).[53] The fostering of such an impression may serve as a Pynchonian, rather than Pynchonesque, commentary on the numbing quality of contemporary American life, the shadow of which, in the novel, is Thanatoid life: "But we watch a lot of Tube" becomes "Uhk ee ahkhh uh akh uh Oomb" (170), if we may be allowed to take this garbled utterance as a synecdochic representation of the relationship between living Americans and Thanatoids, who become distorted beings through their over consumption of television. Watching the Tube is not simply a point of convergence for the two groups, nor merely a characteristic element of the lives of each. Rather, Thanatoid watching is an imprecise, because mostly passive, repetition of American watching. "There'll never be a Thanatoid sitcom [. . .] 'cause all they could show'd be scenes of Thanatoids watchin' the Tube!" (171); a yearly televised Thanatoid Roast is the only thinkable possibility—an idea that is itself presented as a joke during a Thanatoid Roast (220)—that they'll end up on the active side of the screen. American life, by contrast, attempts or hopes, at least partially, to join tube-rhythms and become fit for television: "Be all right again soon. [. . .] Only a couple more commercials, just hold on, Prair" (105) illustrates a typical approach to the world. The extreme version of this tendency is expressed in Hector Zuñiga, whose tubal addiction feeds his dependence on the "Tubal fantasies about his profession" (345) that "ke[ep] him going" (344) while simultaneously distancing him from what is truly important to his life, his ability to enjoy the love he feels for his wife,[54] much as heroin addiction in *Inherent Vice* is a barrier to participating in a loving relationship.[55]

Whether or not *Vineland*'s exploration of the influence of television on American life is meant to serve as a critique,[56] the tube presides over the novel not simply because it is a medium in which characters' lives have become immersed but also because of the role played by Takeshi, who is, or was, a character in a television show: his last appearance in Pynchon's fiction before *Vineland*, that is, the last time we hear about him in *Gravity's Rainbow*, is as one half of the comical kamikaze duo in "a seventh rerun of the Takeshi and Ichizo Show" (738). The answer to the implied question behind DL's statement "I can't imagine you in anybody's air force, let alone the kamikaze, who, I understand from the history books, were fairly picky about who flew for 'em" (175), is that his role shaded into fiction, the televised comedic variety. Takeshi reappears in *Vineland* as the outlaw, the Badass writ small, or the agent "of the poor [or preterite, who is . . .] more skilled and knowledgeable in the arts of karmic readjustment" (xi), as Pynchon puts it in his introduction to Jim Dodge's *Stone Junction* (1990, 1997), than us average folk. DL is "still finding out what he could do. And couldn't" (100), and she later notes, "I know he's got all kinds of people after him, and some others he won't even tell me about. For years now, I've been his accomplice in . . . I don't know what you'd call it, a life of international crime?" (381). Takeshi may be left in the background for much of the novel, but he serves as its spirit, or daemon, opening up the path through which Prairie's plotline moves forward: his business card, the giri chit (100), brings Prairie into contact with DL and, in turn, the information DL and those she is in touch with from 24fps can provide to piece together Frenesi's story, the majority of the one we, Pynchon's readers, learn. He also comes forward to whisk Prairie away from danger, keeping her out of Vond's hands, allowing her investigation to continue, and providing her with the opportunity to reunite with her mother.

His own investigating days having come to an end, Takeshi's skill in karmic adjustment lies in his ability, both with Prairie and among the Thanatoids, to facilitate his clients' investigations into the stories they need to resolve, enabling them to direct their narratives into healthier paths. Hence, despite his warning against seeking revenge, Takeshi "run[s] traces on" (174) those whom Ortho Bob would exact it on, but he notes, "Death, in Modern Karmic Adjustment, got removed from the process" (175). "The cycles of birth and death" (174) had proved too slow, giving rise instead to a market in information and giving hope to those in the present, because while it had sometimes taken centuries for a balance to be found, these days "[t]he amount of memory on a chip doubles every year and a half!" Still, "[t]he state of the art will only allow this to move so fast!" (174). The doppelganger of Vond, Takeshi, gathers information not to control those informing and those informed against in what N. Katherine Hayles calls the "snitch system" (15) but to return control to those who have lost it.

The question asked in the novel may be "Who was saved?" (29), but the question posed by the novel is How do we use what we know or can learn to resolve the failure that left few, if any, saved so that we can get past the inertia that returned in the wake of the counterculture's collapse and establish an environment, at least on a personal level, in which hope can be fostered? Through raising this question, Pynchon writes himself into the novel as a Karmic Adjustment agent, but the art he fashions—meant to enable us to take control of our place in the narrative of the day—can only enable things to move so fast, even in the Computer Age when "all the cats are jumping out of all the bags and even beginning to mingle [. . ., when a]nybody with the time, literacy and access fee [. . .] can get together with just about any piece of specialized knowledge s/he may need" ("Luddite" 169). It's not simply, as David Porush puts it, whether "machinery and metaphor collaborate [. . .] in service of darkness or light" (42); it's that they collaborate for either darkness or light depending on who is in control. There are the Vonds, who offer (to return to the *Stone Junction* introduction) "the threat, indeed promise, of control without mercy that lay in wait down the comely vistas of freedom that computer-folk were imagining" (xii), and there are the Takeshis, the outlaws who may find a way to guide us to such comely vistas. But even if the latter prove incapable of doing so, there is, as Maxine notes in a different context, "never going to be recourse for you in the straight world. The only help you'll find now will be from some kind of outlaw" (*BE* 175).

III

Pynchon seems to have hoped the Sixties had the potential to move the country beyond its tendency to accept stasis, a hope, he recognized, that had been undercut within the period and finally faded away with the rise of eighties culture, when, to use the terms established in *Vineland*, "the Nixonian Reaction" (*Vl* 239) came to be so assimilated into the cultural norm that young people, usually regarded as a source of hope in Pynchon's writing, started "comín in all on their own [around 1981] askín about careers" (347) as undercover agents, or snitches. The important year, symbolically speaking, is 1984, thanks partly to George Orwell but also, perhaps, to biographical events. That was the year *Slow Learner* appeared, with an autobiographical introduction that offers, along with the deprecating commentary on Pynchon's early stories, a quasi-positive take on the present, one in which Pynchon can still, if somewhat anachronistically as *Vineland* evidences, tout the benefits of marijuana and assert "rock 'n' roll will never die" (23). The introduction is, at least in part, about why we should be glad things—cultural and, in relation to Pynchon's own work anyway, literary—are no longer the way they were back in the 1950s. One cultural point is highlighted in the discussion of the end of "The Small Rain," where, Pynchon notes, "some kind of sexual encounter appears to take place, though you'd never know it from the text. The language suddenly gets too fancy to read." Explaining, even justifying, that obscurity, Pynchon goes on to write, "I think, looking back, that there might have been a general nervousness [about sex] in the whole college-age subculture. A tendency to self-censorship. [. . .] Today," he asserts, "this all seems a dead issue, but back then it was a felt constraint on folks's writing" (6).

The issue of confining oneself to print-appropriate language, Pynchon would soon discover, wasn't quite yet dead. After writing the *Slow Learner* introduction, he found himself battling the entrenched conservatism of the *New York Times Book Review*, which pulled "Is It O.K. to Be a Luddite?" from its pages just as the issue in which it was originally set to appear was ready to print. The problem, Rebecca Sinkler reports (69), was Abe Rosenthal, the executive editor; he considered the word "badass" too vulgar for the paper and wanted it removed. Pynchon, objecting to being censored, refused to find a more acceptable term. He won his battle with Rosenthal: the essay was published in the *Book Review* of October 28, 1984, with the "offensive" term in place. But being asked to censor himself may have been a problem in itself, reminding Pynchon of his youthful self-repression and serving as one more sign that the gains of the Sixties were too quickly being taken away or had never been grasped in their full potential.[57] *Slow Learner*'s introduction suggests as much. There, tying literary failures to cultural failures, Pynchon connects his generation's limited success in taking advantage of the divergent directions in fiction that emerging voices were showing them they could take with the limited nature of the success of the "'new left' later in the '60s," noting that he and his contemporaries did not understand that they should have been "groping after a synthesis," and recalling, in the sentence that follows, the "failure of college kids and blue-collar workers to get together politically" (7).[58]

The problem manifests itself in *Vineland* in the allegorical struggle over Frenesi, who, in one sense, "embodies the 1960s," as Dieter Meindl points out (202). The struggle is not the one between Weed, the problematic and therefore doomed representative of the counterculture, and Vond, the archetypal establishment figure; it is the one between Vond and Sasha/Zoyd, a combination of the old left, which sees the counterculture as "stupid potheads" (297), or "hippie bums" (304), and the counterculture, which doesn't necessarily acknowledge the importance of the old fight, as evidenced by Zoyd's "working gypsy construction jobs" when he met Frenesi and by his "scab activities" (319), as his ex-in-laws call his working such jobs, once he settles in Vineland. Even in the face of a common enemy, Sasha and Zoyd are initially unable to cooperate. Zoyd, attempting to enlist Sasha in his cause, is rebuffed as if he were another adversary: "I'm not going to fink on my own daughter" (58), Sasha declares, leaving Zoyd to call attention to their common cause: "OK then, how about Brock Vond, who we both know for what he is, exactly the kind of criminal fascist you've been takin' honest shots at all your life—are you gonna be loyal to somebody like that?" (58). They are, in any case, unable to save Frenesi. She has already flown back to Vond, having failed at being a genuine leftist revolutionary, despite her continued commitment, in some respects, to the old left's ideals—as revealed by her refusal to cross a picket line after years of working for the forces her upbringing taught her to oppose. She is incapable of synthesizing, as needs to be done, old and new, and remains, despite appearances, "so inappropriate" (56), as Sasha realizes, for the period's countercultural opposition.

Sasha and Zoyd finally agree, despite their mutual distrust, to establish a truce for the sake of Prairie. They understand that "no judge would waste the time deciding whose rap sheet was more disreputable—if it was a choice between a lifelong Red grandmother and a dope fiend father, Prairie would end up as a ward of the court [something akin to what becomes of Frenesi], and no question, they had to keep her out of that" (57). The indifference of the authorities to the distinction between different forms of opposition prompts a compromise.

Vineland County, a refuge for the hippies and a place with a history tied to America's leftist past, serves as a geographical metaphor for that compromise: it is a place where the next generation can be sheltered from fascist control but where those affiliated with the left of the late sixties and members of earlier leftist movements remain unable to unite. They merely come to tolerate each other, while the children develop their own modes of opposition, approaching conventional cultural forms through parody. These parodies, however, come across for the children presenting them, if not for the narrator, as unintentional, as earnest attempts by the young to reconcile themselves to the world in which they will come of age. Isaiah's dream of establishing a Disney-like chain of "violence centers, each on the scale, perhaps, of a small theme park," meant to attract a "family clientele" (19) is a mistakenly—not, at least from the character's perspective, sarcastically—skewered presentation of a so-called acceptable American cultural form. The reader may wonder if Isaiah's idea is a Disneyfication of punk or a punkification of Disney.

Pynchon simultaneously celebrates and questions the value of Sixties' social movements, hence the ambiguity of *Vineland*'s PR[3] as well as the double, contradictory significance of Denis's name and of Coy and Hope's existence in *Inherent Vice*. Such ambiguity can be taken to connote that those involved in the period's countercultural movements were, as Pynchon represents them, caught in America's stagnant state, something Doc draws attention to while musing about the involvement of the Golden Fang in the heroin trade and the rehabilitation industry[59]: "Get them coming and going, twice as much revenue and no worries about new customers—as long as American life was something to be escaped from, the cartel could always be sure of a bottomless pool of new customers" (192). Whether one has gone, dropped out, or come, returned to the fold—or perhaps the order is reversed in Doc's mind—one can't escape the culture in which "[f]rom the time we were little kids, they brainwashed us all with all kinds of jive about how lucky America was, is and will continue to be, world without end, amen, and how lucky we were to be living in it. They taught us Dr. Johnson's line ass backward, that there's much to be enjoyed, little to be endured, and we, saps and too young to know better, believed it" (quoted in Siegel 1970 186). In *The Crying of Lot 49*, Oedipa comes to think of the culture as one characterized by "the exitlessness, [...] the absence of surprise to life, that harrows the head of everybody American you know" (170). It is the culture that the Golden Fang facilitates "a progressive *knotting into*" (*GR* 3). That organization therefore serves as a negative of *Lot 49*'s Tristero, a network that supports "a disentanglement from" (*GR* 3) such monotony, revealing, if not "a real alternative" (*CL49* 170), the possibility of alternatives. The revelation is evident whichever of the four hypotheses about the Tristero's origin that Oedipa posits near the novel's end turns out to be true, for it is through her investigation of the Tristero that she becomes aware that exits are conceivable.

From the start, Oedipa treats the Tristero network as "a secret richness and concealed density of dream" (170) and continues to do so after positing her symmetrical hypotheses, something evinced by her showing up at the auction (as the novel ends) prepared to cause "a scene violent enough to bring the cops into it" (183), that is, prepared to turn her problem over to the authorities so that the Tristero's deviance can be revealed and brought under control. Her search for the truth of the Tristero, after all, is an attempt to accommodate its existence to her world. She approaches it as an orthodox Freudian, at least as described by Dr. Hilarius, approaches the unconscious, as something that "would be like any other room, once the light was let in. That the dark shapes would resolve into toy horses and Biedermeyer furniture" (135). The shapes don't become manageable. The Tristero functions the same way, or could generate the same effect, whether or not it's a hoax or a delusion. Beyond the possibility that the Tristero is an actual network, at least two of Oedipa's articulated scenarios are shown to be capable of producing the alienating effects that Oedipa suffers for believing it is one: Dr. Hilarius's belief in an Israeli threat corresponds to Oedipa's fantasizing the whole thing, and he is taken away in a straitjacket, a confirmed lunatic; and the alteration LSD produces in Mucho corresponds to Oedipa's fear that she is hallucinating her encounter with the Tristero. (Drugs aren't simply, as Cowart writes, "to *Vineland* what the Tristero is to *Lot 49*" [98]; they are to Mucho what the Tristero is to Oedipa.)

The possibility that Oedipa has become a pawn in an elaborate plot orchestrated by Pierce may also have its analogue in Metzger's "elaborate, seduction, plot" (31), which, beyond seeming the logical "starting point for" her discovery of the Tristero, serves in a way as a microcosm of the macrocosmic plot, hinting at the doubleness that Oedipa will discover in American culture. The seduction takes place before a television, well established by the 1960s as "a medium of hopeless consensus" (1), as Lynn Spigel and Michael Curtin observe, just as the movie industry had been, Oedipa assumes, an homogenized medium: "All those movies had happy endings" (34), she notes, implicitly associating them, because of their sameness, with her "fat deckful of days which seemed [...] more or less identical" (11). Metzger gets her to admit "all" is really "most," and *Cashiered*—the movie on the local station that replaces NBC's family-oriented *Bonanza* (1959-1973) in Oedipa's evening plans—proves to be among the exceptions, much as was the night Pierce called the last time she spoke with him and as is this evening, during which Metzger develops the game "Strip Botticelli" (36) and Oedipa strips off, layer after layer, her life's attire. The suggestion here may be that television had the possibility of offering access to alternative narratives, at the local level if not at the national level, where success depends on the creation of a homogenized audience, something that links the major networks, by analogy, to the Golden Fang and thus heroin addiction.[60] Pynchon hence notes in *Vineland*, "Minute the Tube got hold of you folks that was it, that whole alternative America, el deado meato" (373). Developing the medium so that it would accommodate itself to a national stage undermined the hope it could have given, not because communal unity is necessarily negative but because the type of communal unity is grounded in distraction, or mindless pleasures, as Mucho realizes: "Give us too much to process, fill up every minute, keep us distracted, it's what the Tube is for, and though it kills me to say it, it's what rock and roll is becoming—just another way to claim our attention" (*VL* 314).[61]

Whatever the status of the seduction may be—a starting point for Oedipa's discovery, a microcosmic representation of it, or both—the world from which Oedipa has come, the one "mothered over" by "Secretaries James [Forrestal] and [John] Foster and Senator Joseph" McCarthy, has been left on "another pattern of track" (104). The reference here is to Oedipa's college years on the Cornell campus of the 1950s—when "[o]ne year [. . .] was much like another" (*SL* 14)—a campus so unlike the Berkeley of 1964 that Oedipa observes.[62] An allusion to her recent life—her Tupperware, Republican milieu with its seemingly identical days—is also present. Oedipa's married life was as deeply conformist as her college one, but both are, for her, "impossible to find ever again" (104). Her marriage therefore ends, as we learn in *Vineland*, in an amicable divorce, implying that the disenfranchised, Mucho now also among them, are splintered but nonetheless share a common position. The Cornell Oedipa attended is also the one Pynchon attended.

He is around Oedipa's age, and his Cornell, although "doing its duty to act *in loco parentis*" (Introduction to *Been Down So Long* vii) by imposing strict curfews and doing its best to curtail erotic activity among students, was not always as bleak as Oedipa recalls: The university's "extraordinary meddling was not seriously protested until the Spring of 1958," when "like a preview of the '60s, students got together on the issue, wrote letters, rallied, demonstrated, and finally, a couple of thousand strong, by torchlight in the curfew hours between May 23rd and 24th, marched to and stormed the home of the University president" (vii), as Pynchon recalls in his introduction to Fariña's *Been Down So Long It Looks Like Up to Me* (1966). Pynchon's "not seriously" suggests there were small gestures of rebellion before the May events, just as the "widely and immediately recognized [odor of marijuana smoke the day revolution reached *Vineland's* College of the Surf] later led historians of the incident to question the drug innocence of this student body" (205). Oedipa's world had never been as conformist as she thought it; she just hadn't been very attentive to her surroundings.

If that Cornell protest was like a preview, an early appearance of the light that would later fill the parenthesis, the significance of its visibility remained unclear—either because broadening awareness of the events, at least as Pynchon asks us to envision them in his introduction to Fariña's novel (see vii), came by way of rumor or because those events would appear only retroactively as a preview to anything, much as Pynchon's belief that Fariña "caught something" "in the guitar break of ['Peggy Sue'] [. . .], some flash of things to come" is likely a "retro-fantasy" (ix). The significance of the protest, as Pynchon understands it looking back, was like the "sunrise over the library slope at Cornell" (10) that Oedipa recalls but that no one, including Oedipa, had faced because everyone was looking the wrong way.[63] To return to Oedipa's track metaphor, divergent patterns were being laid down even if some were not clearly seen: Oedipa has left the one made by Senator McCarthy and his ilk in favor of the one to which her encounter with the Tristero has led her. She has wandered onto a track "beyond the appearance of the legacy America," a beyond that Oedipa comes to recognize must exist even if "there was just America," for "if there was just America then it seemed the only way she could continue, and manage to be at all relevant to it, was as an alien" (182), that is, as a member of another world, the presence of which her investigation of the Tristero has enabled her, if not to find for the first time,[64] to recognize as an alternative position from which to project herself into America or observe what has been projected.

That other world—filled with individuals and groups that may be, but are not necessarily, connected through W.A.S.T.E—is one where the Peter Pinguid Society has leaned so far Right that it is against Industrial Capitalism; where squatters stay along railroad tracks, in abandoned freight cars, "behind smiling billboards along" highways, and "in junkyards [. . .] or [. . .] up some pole in a lineman's tent"; where drifters, Americans, speak "their [alternative] language carefully, scholarly, as if they were in exile from somewhere else invisible yet congruent with the cheered land [Oedipa] lived in" (180); where inventors attempt to reestablish their individuality beyond a culture of teamwork; where an underworld of failed suicides communicate their despair; where isolates maintain a society that is held together by the members' separation from each other; where children live through their dreams in the urban night; where anarchists distribute their literature, perhaps since the century's start; where death cults attempt to find converts among the disenfranchised and find victims among the well-adjusted; where misfits prepare for the day that dolphins will displace humans; where an African-American woman reiterates a ritual of miscarriage; and where numerous others, subjected to a variety of different "alienations await their inheritance, even though they have surely "forgotten by now what it [is]" (180).

Oedipa's entrance into the cultural moment referred to as the Sixties is enacted on the tracks at the end of the novel, an idea emphasized by *Inherent Vice*. As Scott McClintock observes, "The sentence, 'Behind the hieroglyphic streets there would either be a transcendent meaning or only the earth,' is recalled in *Inherent Vice* in the epigraph to the novel, 'Under the paving stones, the beach!' which is graffito from the 1968 student rebellion in France" (108). We might add that the possible existence of AC-DC, or the Alameda County Death Cult, in the world of *Lot 49* prefigures Charles Manson's cult, the existence of which haunts the world of *Inherent Vice*. We might also add that for those behind the hieroglyphic streets, the communication on those streets, that which comes from the "cheered land," registers only as "the dumb voltages flickering their miles, the night long, in the thousands of unheard messages" (180). The voices of those inhabiting the surface world are to those who belong to the underground what the voices Oedipa is "beginning to [...] listen to" (*SL* 22), to borrow from Pynchon's description of his own development, were to her in her sheltered existence in Kinneret-Among-The-Pines. Those on either side of the divide listen to those on the other without full comprehension, although those inhabiting the underworld may better comprehend those who inhabit the surface world. For instance, "A Watts kid," Pynchon observes, "knows more of what goes on inside white heads than possibly whites do themselves; knows how often the little man has looked at him and thought, 'Bad credit risk'—or 'Poor learner,' or 'Sexual threat,' or 'Welfare chiseler'—without knowing a thing about him personally" ("JMW" 80).

The correspondences between *The Crying of Lot 49* and *Inherent Vice* suggest that the two novels are parallel works in Pynchon's fictional oeuvre: Oedipa is the counterpart to

Doc, finding herself on the threshold of the parenthesis, whose light may have first begun to appear during that Cornell sunrise from which everyone was looking away, but attempting to keep what it will contain, or what may always have been underneath the Republic's surface, at bay. The "central truth" she sets out to find is meant to satisfy, as Cyrus R. K. Patell puts it, "a desire for order and significance at all costs, a desire above all to be 'inside, safe' instead of 'outside, lost'" (130). Doc, on the threshold of the exit, strives to counter the Golden Fang's insinuation of itself into the alternatives. The moment Doc comes to see the cartel's hold on both America's mainstream and its countercultural life, he presents himself as one who may be capable of finding a way out of the impasse the Golden Fang seems capable of manipulating for its own advantage, telling Coy, "if I did just run a fast check and happened to find some angle you maybe haven't thought of—" (192).

Doc has already proved capable of facilitating such an escape, though on a smaller scale, saving himself, Denis, and Jade/Ashley from the pursuit of the zombies, whose presence at the Boards' residence ought to remind us of Mucho's remark in *Vineland* about what "rock and roll" is becoming and also of *Vineland*'s Thanatoids, even though they are the negative of zombies. The Thanatoids are who and/or what they are, in part, because they have been pacified; the distraction offered by television is symbolic of that pacification, a condition some among the living, those who "discover they were already Thanatoids without knowing it" (384; for the television connection, see McHale 118), also suffer. Zombies, by contrast, are the media-in-pursuit-of-pacification, a logical part of the Golden Fang, the implied presence of which at The Boards' house—implied by Coy's taking up residence there—suggests it is co-opting not just drug use but rock 'n' roll, the growing superficiality of which as a subversive force has earlier been made manifest in the audition booths of Wallach's Music City as well as by Mucho in *Vineland*.[65] The zombie episode also establishes a connection between the threshold on which *Inherent Vice*'s world is situated and the underworld, a connection that is both mythical—in the sense that it is connected with the dead—and criminal—in that a criminal enterprise is, to use a metaphor from the drug trade, stepping on every aspect of American life.[66]

It is as a liberator that Doc assumes the role of Dionysus, one of the few figures in Greek mythology to successfully return someone—his mother, Semele—from the underworld (Otto 67), at least in one tradition. In another tradition, he is associated with Persephone, even as her son, delivering his initiates from the punishment associated with the underworld (Edmonds 56–61): "Dionysus is responsible for deliverance," an Orphic fragment cited by Damascius reads, "and for this very reason the god is called Deliverer"(quoted in Graf and Iles Johnston 132). Indeed, the very nature of Doc's profession is Dionysian, at least as he pursues or tries to pursue it, accounting for his ability to participate "in the same business" as Bigfoot (26) and the FBI (74) and yet to separate himself, as much as possible, from its negative elements, despite the doubts about his doing so that Shasta raises near the novel's end. These doubts lead him to recall those cases that seem to place his career on the Apollonian side of things, cases that involved binding the principals, Japonica chief among them, to worlds they would be better off escaping. The most obvious instance of Doc's serving as a Dionysian PI is in his looking into Coy's supposed death and enabling Coy's return to Hope. Hope, however, isn't there for everyone. "Glen Charlock is still dead" (258). Wolfmann's return, as well as his disappearance, is brought about through the offices of the Feds[67] and the Golden Fang, and he reassumes the role he had played before he set out to undermine the workings of the straight world with his plan to provide free real estate. Shasta, meanwhile, is back at the beach, looking as if she had never left: she is neither saved nor damned, the reader, like Doc, being left unsure what to think.

Being unsure what to think is part of the process of coming to terms with Pynchon's take on the Sixties, as well as the America that has emerged since its passing. Thus *Inherent Vice* closes with Doc driving through the fog similar to "the falling dark and confusion without limit" (*Vl* 244) that descends upon the College of the Surf as the PR[3] falls apart. The fog's darkness, however, is different. It may blind those on the highway to what is ahead, but the blindness leads them, in Doc's imagination if not in reality, to "set up a temporary commune[, hippie-like,] to help each other home" (*IV* 368), a commune that is a product of something akin to the nostalgia "alumni associations" (368) use to get members to gather and remember. That such reminiscences would be facilitated not in the world available to Doc but in the one available to us, "with phones as standard equipment in every car, maybe even dashboard computers" (368), implies that once the fog lifts, or the novel ends, Doc's era will have come to a close. The realization is not a hopeless one, for the insertion of twenty-first-century technology into Doc's fantasy draws our attention to the possibility of our seeing through the fog, if only we would attend to the advantages of that technology with a spirit more akin to Doc's than, for example, to that of *Bleeding Edge*'s Gabriel Ice.

Less figuratively, both *Vineland* and *Inherent Vice* ask us to construct an opposition between the forces of freedom and the forces of control, but the characters, Vond excepted, who are apparently meant to represent one or the other side of that opposition often find themselves positioned on both sides simultaneously. For instance, *Vineland*'s Hector, due to his tubal addiction, comes to play in Frenesi's narrative, admittedly in a smaller way, the same role Takeshi plays in Prairie's narrative. He guides Frenesi, as Takeshi guides Prairie, to the place where she can return to her family and thereby allows her to reconnect with her leftist roots. Hector, too, is an outlaw, incipiently from the moment he arrived in Zoyd's life "with the outlaw hat and cop sideburns" (23) and who is now on the lam, seeking to develop a documentary outside official channels, albeit one meant to forward the day's antidrug hysteria, which he has been able to manipulate to get funding. Determining what side he is on, as opposed to which one he believes he is on, is a dizzying task because his approach to serving the powers that be undercuts their control. The breakdown of the Dionysian/Apollonian opposition is more pointed in *Inherent Vice*. Doc might be a Dionysian PI, but he can't completely separate himself from the Apollonian elements of his profession: hence the import of Shasta's characterization of him as a "co[p] who never wanted to be [a] co[p]" (313) and Chastity Bjornsen's moniker for him, "Mr. Moral Turpitude" (260). (What exactly, we might ask, is Bigfoot telling his wife about Doc?) Similarly, the cops are not fully Apollonian. The culture of law enforcement is held together by a Dionysian element, "[t]he bond between partners," which "was nearly the only thing that Doc had ever found to admire about the LAPD" (66).

Such a bond comes to tie the novel's strands together, uniting Doc to Bigfoot in a relationship that is only superficially antagonistic. Almost the first thing we learn about Bigfoot is that he is Doc's "old cop budd[y]" (8). Doc deflects the characterization, observing that Bigfoot would more likely arrest him than help him. The next morning, we learn that Bigfoot has been looking for him, something Doc tries to portray as a pursuit: "Why didn't he just kick my door down like he usually does?" (13). Bigfoot never actually kicks Doc's door down—except at the end of the movie adaptation, where the action is a prelude to his joining Doc's world, if only momentarily, and embracing his own freakish interior as he consumes a significant amount of pot and takes Denis's part in dialogue taken from the novel, something that "leaves the viewer wondering," as I have noted elsewhere, "if Bigfoot is a sort of hippie freak who never wanted to be a hippie freak" (Rolls 2014). His reasons for looking for Doc are not related to harassing him for criminal behavior. If they were, he could have brought up the subject after Charlock's murder, when he has Doc in custody. What is going on at this early point is probably closer to what goes on between the two after Doc returns from Vegas, when Bigfoot is again looking for him.

Bigfoot calls Doc, evidently not for the first time over the days Doc has been away, to check in on him after his being impossible to find. "You know how anxious we get" (259), Bigfoot observes. The observation seems, on first reading, aggressive, that of a cop frustrated by not knowing Doc's (or a suspect's) whereabouts, but in light of Bigfoot's warning the following morning that Doc doesn't "want to be fucking with this" (264), meaning the case of Coy's staged death, it takes on the air of genuine concern, albeit somewhat concealed. The exchange leading up to the warning is one Doc seems to want to avoid. Upon hearing that Bigfoot is looking for him, he heads out of Wavos's back door, an attempt to slip away, we are led to believe, but the lieutenant is waiting. Bigfoot immediately turns on his cop routine, declaring "I'm not planning to inflict bodily harm" and then blaming his abstaining from violence on the era's influence on him: "Part of this godforsaken hippie era and its erosion of masculine values I expect" (263). Bigfoot, in effect, calls attention to his affinity to and for Doc, who starts in on his harassed-victim routine, acting as if he needs to worry about getting shot. The prop he uses, the Wyatt Earp mustache cup that he brought Bigfoot from Vegas, undercuts the seriousness of his fears. (The gift evinces that they really are "buddies.") The two then exchange nervous apologies about the phone call the previous night, clearly demonstrating their emotional investment in each other and their clichéd masculine inability to express it. They may obscure to themselves the strength of their bond, but not to Sauncho, who grasps the significance of their banter early on, when Doc is in custody. Describing their back-and-forth as "embarrassing," Sauncho—who homonymically plays interpretive sidekick to any quixotic reader who buys into the surface fiction of Doc and Bigfoot's mutual antipathy—remarks, "Maybe you two should find somewhere besides an interrogation cubicle" (30).

The reason Bigfoot has been looking for Doc near the novel's end is to update him on new developments, the death of El Drano: the meeting is one Doc must have expected on some level, or he wouldn't have brought Bigfoot's gift. Holding such meetings is part of a pattern: throughout the novel, the two continually look for each other to share or seek information about cases, the value of which cooperation is highlighted by contrast with Doc's seemingly pointless visit to Lieutenant Dubonnet to inquire about Coy. Doc and Bigfoot have become, in effect, partners, something Paul Thomas Anderson calls attention to when he has Adrian Prussia, in a line that is original to the movie, remark to Bigfoot about Doc, "This your new partner?" (57). Prussia is being sarcastic, mocking Bigfoot, but both the denotative meaning and the sarcastic intent of the comment are to the point. Doc and Bigfoot may coordinate their efforts, but they do so in a backhand manner, as if they themselves can't believe they are working with each other. Hence Doc asks,

"Where'd be the nameless, unspoken-of-partner to watch Doc's back for him?" (285) when he is looking through Indelicato's file, and the novel answers with Bigfoot, who is close by when Puck Beaverton holds Doc prisoner and when Doc exchanges the heroin for Coy.

Conscious intimacy, however, is off limits, so when Doc attempts to reach past the surface shtick and find out about Bigfoot's private life, asking whether he has a wife and kids, to discover what *Vineland* refers to (albeit sarcastically) as the "cops-are-only-human-got-to-do-their-job" story (345),[68] Bigfoot keeps up the mask, remarking, "I hope this isn't some kind of veiled hippie threat" (32). For Bigfoot, he and Doc should be involved only in what Pynchon in his Watts essay calls "a ritual exchange" (80), the rules of which Doc has broken. Bigfoot then tries to destroy the dynamic of their partner-like relationship by attempting to recruit Doc as a paid informant and thereby reinforcing the ritual formality that has been breaking down as they grow closer. Doc responds to the cop, not the man he has just sought to learn about, and for the moment allows the ritual to proceed as expected: "Nothing personal, but yours is the last wallet I'd ever want money out of" (33). The partnership seems always to be on the cusp of breaking down as well as of solidifying. Bigfoot isn't Doc's brother, nor is Doc the keeper Bigfoot needs, though it is "[t]oo bad, in a way" (350), as Doc tells Denis, the only time Doc allows his relationship to Bigfoot to be seen by his friends as anything other than antagonistic. Each thus holds back as well as gives, particularly when information is involved. For instance, Doc never mentions Shasta's visit to him about Wolfmann nor his own talk with Puck in Vegas, while Bigfoot suggests with his warning that he knows more than he is saying and, of course, never reveals anything about his murdered partner. Rather, he provides clues that direct Doc where to look.

The relationship works or, to be more precise, becomes a working relationship when it needs to be one. Neither Doc nor Bigfoot may solve the main cases, Charlock's murder and Wolfmann's disappearance, which weren't, considering the involvement of the FBI and the Golden Fang/Vigilant California, really cases, or cases to be solved, to begin with[69] and which Bigfoot himself may be more closely involved with than he is able to let on, as Doc's chat with Art Tweedle (see 201–202) reveals. But each wraps up a separate, more or less related, case with the help of the other. Bigfoot guides Doc to Prussia, enabling Doc to exact for him the kind of extrajudicial justice that only an outlaw can. In return, Bigfoot enables Doc to rescue Coy from the Golden Fang, putting in Doc's possession the twenty kilos of the Golden Fang's heroin that can be exchanged for Coy's freedom. Bigfoot's involvement here confirms Doc's fears not only about his profession but about his era, which he links and contrasts with the era of screen PIs *vis-à-vis* Garfield's career. "PIs are doomed," at least as they once were—that is, as independents, outside the system, who bring to those within it what they need to know—or as we have been taught to think about them via what we have seen on screen, from which all Doc's examples come, examples he contrasts with recent television cops: "Once there was all these great old PIs—[. . .] always end up solvin the crime while the cops are followin wrong leads and gettin in the way" (97).

Resolving the situation Coy finds himself in follows a process that inverts the one for which Doc feels nostalgia. While Doc is the only one who is willing to try to save Coy, he is the one running around with no real idea about what to do, and it is Bigfoot who steps in with the solution, becoming a cop who not only is, in this instance in any case, "no more threat to nobody's freedom than some dad in a sitcom" (97) but who also is, if not a liberator, a facilitator of liberation, sharing with Doc what Hector shares with Takeshi. That Bigfoot's presence is necessary for Doc to succeed—just as Hector's presence, as well as Takeshi's, is necessary for Prairie to connect with Frenesi—is telling. Pynchon recognizes that a pure adherence to the Dionysian principle is as problematic as a rigorous acceptance of the Apollonian principle. Rigorous adherence to either principle alone leaves one unliberated, caught in a mode of being from which escape is necessary. Japonica's problem, for instance, is that she may escape her father but does not find liberation. She merely exchanges her repressive home for milieus of excess, Blatnoyd's milieu in the novel's present. Doc's dealing with her is, therefore, morally ambiguous; a situation into which to deliver her is lacking. That is also, in a sense, the problem Oedipa faces at the end of *Lot 49*, which may be why she considers getting the police involved. Her situation, nonetheless, is more positive than Japonica's. Oedipa's having become aware of the possibility of escape seems to be enough. Japonica, by contrast, needs to find a space of liberation into which to escape.

Pynchon's fiction, from at least *Lot 49* to *Inherent Vice*, shifts from an emphasis on finding a means of escape to an emphasis on achieving liberation. The development seems personal. Pynchon, after all, aligns himself early in his career with Oedipa—whom we watch negotiate the process of breaking out of her tower—via their similar ages and educations and maybe their shared Republican backgrounds, even though Pynchon's high-school publications suggest he became interested in leftist politics before going to college.[70] In the eighties, he figures himself in the guise of a Takeshi— as both lack fixed addresses and are tangentially connected to Northern California, where Pynchon spent some time in the mid-seventies as well as the mid-eighties.[71] Takeshi provides those willing to go to him the perspective they need to see the stories they are bound to in ways that allow them to fashion their own exits from the karmic traps in which they are caught. Pynchon, in 2009, presents himself as Doc—whose voice he furnishes for *Inherent Vice*'s book trailer—a somewhat settled-down liberator—"You know I have an office now? just like a day job and everything?" (*IV* 1)—who makes it his job to cure those he works for of their need to remain trapped, reworking, as he does with Coy, their positions within the narratives they believe they must live.

A positive synthesis of the Dionysian and Apollonian, in the terminology that *Inherent Vice* suggests we use, has been achieved, perhaps the one Pynchon felt he had neglected earlier in his career (see *SL* 7), when the terminology he would likely have used was Romanticism and Classicism. At the time, he imagined "his autobiography sharing with literary history this structuring, countervailing pull of two superpowers—Romanticism and Classicism—locked in a great war" (697), Steven Weisenburger observes in his discussion of the autobiographical sketch Pynchon wrote for the statement of purpose he submitted to the Ford Foundation in 1959.[72] The conflict, readers who have paid attention to Pynchon's appearances in the press might think, has been a lifelong struggle. He "is more than highbrow," Chrissie Wexler described him to James Bone in the 1990s; "[h]e is the highest of browcries," she went on. Yet writing to celebrate his friend Phyllis Gebauer's donation to UCLA of books he had signed for her, Pynchon joked as if he were still in Manhattan Beach, hanging out with the types to whom Doc might find himself passing joints: "I was planning to skydive into the middle of these proceedings. [. . .] Thank you for your teaching. Good work and good vibes to everybody there" (quoted in Kellogg).

Considering the Enclave

PYNCHON'S engagement with the Classical–Romantic[73] duality may appear to involve a back-and-forth dynamic in the Ford Foundation statement of purpose, but the dynamic comes across as less simple not just in such late works as *Inherent Vice*, a novel in which a synthesis, as we have seen, is sought after, but also in some of Pynchon's early writings, particularly those not written with publication in mind. It's not that an early synthesis can be found; it's that Pynchon seems to feel the need to distance himself from the position on whichever side of the divide he appears to be taking. In a letter written to Kirkpatrick Sale and Sale's then-girlfriend Patricia Mahool early in 1959, for instance, Pynchon illustrates what he would later call his "adopting Beat postures and props" (9), a characterization of his younger self in the *Slow Learner* introduction that suggests he is looking back on himself with a mixture of bemusement and embarrassment. But he had already developed a complicated attitude toward the Beats in college. Indeed, what Pynchon writes to Sale and Mahool suggests he was placing himself at an ironic distance from those who sought to imitate the Beats slavishly. Observing that after leaving Queens he "stayed up all night, roaming the negro streets," he adopts the position of those Allen Ginsberg celebrates in "Howl" (1956) and then draws attention to his pretense, adding "specifically penn station and environs," where there may have been "bums" but not "an angry fix" ("Howl" 2). As if to make sure the irony is recognized, he later writes, "I love sick sick sick. [. . .] [Jules] feiffer has this group up here [Greenwich Village hipsters] defined perfectly, pinned to the cork board and fluttering helplessly,"[74] a statement that surely resonated as Eliotic to the young Pynchon, who describes himself as "entrenched on the T. S. Eliot side of no man's land" in the autobiographical sketch that he sent to the Ford Foundation (Weisenburger 697).

Still, ironic retelling aside, no one spends all night among "bums" without maintaining some fascination with the gesture. Such fascination is displayed with more force in the unfinished 1958 musical "Minstrel Island" that Pynchon and Kirkpatrick Sale worked on about six months prior to Pynchon's winter-break trip to New York City, the occasion of his letter to Sale and Mahool. Elements of that work anticipate aspects of Pynchon's published writings, most strikingly the musical's use of an enclave whose inhabitants strive to exist independently of the dominant culture. The island, Camelot, could be viewed as a less complex version of the Vineland into which Zoyd escapes, for example. Pynchon's fashioning of such enclaves illustrates a partiality for his Romantic inclinations despite his misgivings about that literary mode, misgivings that became evident in "Minstrel Island" perhaps only because of the incomplete state of the work and because of the presence of two voices working to converge, an element of the text that enables one to gather an idea of the process of putting it together.

I

"Minstrel Island" pits a small group of bohemians against an IBM-dominated society. The bohemians, occupying an island that has so far remained free of IBM control, are led by Hero, a folksinger and songwriter who thus bears some resemblance to Fariña,[75] and include Jazzman, who, in Pynchon's draft, "need[s] a fix" (Act 1, scene 1); Whore; Bombmaker; Sailmaker; Gambler; Uncle Chauncey, a character who writes children's books and who Pynchon seems to have added as he composed his version of the opening scene[76]; and a chorus. The IBM society is represented by Broad, "regional coordinator for the federal committee on backward areas" (P Act 1, scene 1) and chief secretary to Johnny Badass,[77] the leader in the New York State area; Tube Tester; and two women, referred to as Chicks. They arrive on Camelot to subject it and its citizens to IBM culture. The bohemians, to save their enclave, convince Hero to seduce Broad, sex being capable of rekindling the life-energy—a notion derived from the psychoanalyst Wilhelm Reich—that the IBM-structured system has extinguished. The influence of the Beats' embracing of Reich is obvious. Pynchon, however, does not seem to have been the one who chose to use the Reichian conceit: a parenthetical stage direction suggests that the idea was Sale's and that Pynchon may not have been fully comfortable with introducing it.

A section of dialogue, spoken by Whore, reads in Pynchon's draft,

> Hero. (then big lightbulb goes on.) Hmmm. There's one bit we haven't thought of (eager, all of them). I mean obviously (Kirk's suggested pose) SEX. (childish faces light up faces of chorus). That zombie who seems to be in charge. Don't think I didn't notice [Hero and Broad's flirtatious behavior]. (Act 1, scene 1)

The way Sale's name is introduced here suggests some discontent with the idea, because the collaborator responsible for any particular element of the draft is usually left unnamed. Pynchon twice mentions Sale's name, first in the above passage and then at the opening of Act 1, scene 2, the scene in which Hero begins his wooing of Broad. The opening words in the descriptive paragraph that sets that scene read,

"Setting as Kirk suggests," and the setting partly determines the action and the dialogue as developed by Pynchon. It is in front of the carnie booth that Broad sought to remove, and some of the dialogue revolves around a teddy bear that Hero takes after winning the unmanned game carnival goers once paid to play and that he gives to Broad later in the scene. Pynchon apparently had in mind a different setting and called attention to his agreeing to forget about it by naming Sale in the draft, leaving us to wonder for whom Pynchon wrote these notes: another reader to whom he and Sale planned to show the draft or just Sale? Whatever the specifics might have been, the effect of naming Sale is to distance Pynchon from some of the decisions that were made.[78]

Mere sex, in any case, is replaced by a more romantic conception of love in the scene that comes after the one that introduces Whore's plot, a development that follows the text of Pynchon's outline. The distinction might not register with Broad—who notes that "[l]ove is an archaic word referring to libidinous & almost always sexual stimuli occurring in the pre-civilized human" (P Act 1, scene 2)[79]—but is certainly treated as real in the text. Hero courts rather than seduces Broad, never going beyond kissing her, and he falls for her as much as she falls for him. In Act 3, scene 1, there was to be "some small indication that [Hero] might possibly think of defecting to the ibmers, so great is his love," an idea that, at least initially, suggests Hero misunderstands the IBMers as much as Broad misunderstands love. Defecting to the IBMers, after all, would presumably mean Hero's assuming the role that Johnny Badass seeks to play in Broad's life, joining "his test tubes with her in marriage" (Act 1, scene 3). In the 1998 of "Minstrel Island," marriage does not require exclusivity, for Broad's friends—in the scene in which Johnny Badass's proposal is revealed—simultaneously encourage her to go out on a date with a "mad ave frat boy" and to marry

Johnny Badass. Broad, meanwhile, does not fully comprehend what is happening to her: "she feels a really strange warmth around her heart . . . [and] can't stop thinking of [Hero]" (Act 3, scene 1) but is not yet ready to use the word "love" to describe her feelings. That doesn't happen until Act 3, scene 2—something that Sale mentions in his description of the first scene of that act and that Pynchon's outline confirms—when Broad goes out to find Hero and meets the minstrels. They are leaving without Hero, who has decided to stay, apparently willing to risk living as an IBMer to be with Broad. The minstrels don't tell her what Hero has decided, prompting her to utter, "I love Hero," either to herself or to the minstrels: the outline is unclear on that point.

A secondary plot involving Whore's more Reichian seduction of Tube Tester plays up the distinction between sex and love more forcefully. Whore pursues Tube Tester more lasciviously than Hero ever does Broad, seeking him out at the makeshift offices of Johnny Badass on the island in Act 1, scene 3, embracing him when they meet, and directing his hand to her ass, where it remains until Broad observes what is going on and breaks them up. Whore is intent on using sex to turn Tube Tester, the physicality of her approach reflecting the scheme she urges Hero to follow with Broad, the idea having been expanded to include more IBMers.[80] Whore falls in love, however. That love remains intensely physical, stimulating a relationship that serves as a contrast to the more intellectual connection that undermines Hero and Broad's ability to come together, despite their feelings. Whore's interest in saving the island dissipates as her feelings unexpectedly grow stronger, demonstrating that love wasn't meant to be part of Whore's plan for Hero and Broad. Never thinking she'd "fall [in love] like this," she sings in Sale's provisional "song for prostitute," a song that expresses her change of heart and concludes with her demanding, "Leave us trip the light fantastic/ Down through the meadows, over the hills far away/ [and in Sale's hand] Let us find a small apartment [above which, in Pynchon's hand, is written 'bedroom'] far away." Whore's hope has transformed from a desire to turn the IBMers and save Camelot to a desire to fashion a private enclave—the privacy more strongly emphasized if "apartment" is changed to "bedroom"— into which she and Tube Tester can escape and thus free themselves from IBM's cultural dominance.

Sale's outline ends at that point. Pynchon's outline indicates that there were to be three acts and that the last two scenes, the ones missing from Sale's version, were to revolve around Hero and Broad's clearing up the misunderstanding that arose when Broad stumbled upon the minstrels, including Hero, with one of Bombmaker's devices. That incident leads Broad to turn away from Hero, but a happy ending seems to have been planned. Pynchon's outline implies that they get past their differences and join in the denouement. That happy ending, nonetheless, must have been ambiguous in other ways. The outline of the last scene reads,

> Sc 3) Same scene
> minstrel chorus – leaving songs [An arrow indicates
> this line should be moved down
> to Finale]
> He learns she is to leave w/ JBA for NY
> from pregnant woman
> girl comes + they resolve problems ∞ [maybe "as"] dud bomber
> shows
> IBM – "love" [The words are in the margin; a line indicates they belong above Finale.]
> Finale – everyone except IBM people.

It is difficult to imagine how Hero and Broad's love could produce a situation that would keep the IBMers off the island or undermine the dominant society on any large scale. Broad, after all, doesn't have the influence that the minstrels in Act 1, scene 1, assumed she had, and the island is already IBM occupied by the beginning of Act 2, scene 2. Johnny Badass's returning to New York implies that his work is done and that his presence is no longer necessary. Indeed, Sale's note in his introduction to the play that "[i]t would be a good idea . . . if they [the remnants of the amusement-park stage sets] remained intact for the course of the play" suggests that we should not expect what is left of the amusement park to remain standing after the action of the play concludes.[81] The ineffectualness of Bombmaker's device can even be read as a metonym for the minstrel's fruitless resistance, and its presence proves counterproductive, as it complicates Whore's plan. The outline's note "dud bomber shows" suggests that bombmaker demonstrates that his bomb is more for show than for blowing up things, meaning Broad and Hero resolve their problems by Hero's having Bombmaker demonstrate that the resistance Broad earlier observed was, in fact, mostly aesthetic. The finale with the leaving song stages the minstrel's exit from the island, yet a form of resistance endures.

Whore and Tube Tester's desire to fashion a private refuge presents a more practical and deceptive, because hard-to-recognize, form of defiance, a defiance that involves fashioning something like a beatnik version of the "Paradise within" (*Paradise Lost* XII, 586) that Milton's Adam and Eve retain after their expulsion from Eden. Whore is the perfect vehicle through which to express such a possibility, for she discerns within Broad and Tube Tester the libido that the IBMers have been conditioned to repress and develops the plan to take advantage of it. The IBMers, in short, have within them that which will enable resistance, and Whore is the first to recognize that such is the case. Camelot may be bulldozed and redeveloped, but its spirit will remain active in enclaves that are private rather than geographical, a possibility that not only changes the implications of Hero's decision to join Broad among the IBMers but also foreshadows, if the Milton reference is to the point, a future in which paradise is regained, a time when the values that enable the minstrels to acknowledge that the libido—sexual desire and, although not necessarily, the love that accompanies it—is a positive force. Whore's is a sane response to the inevitable return of the repressed that is evident in the form of a "pregnant woman," as she is called in Pynchon's outline, who appears in Act 1, scene 3, and Act 3, scene 3. In Sale's outline, she rushes into the IBM offices, accusing "the machine of making her pregnant, taking her baby. she is obviously mad" (Act 1, scene 3). The implication is that her being consumed by a desire she was never prepared to cope with has left her unstable, the inevitable end of the IBM social body if it fails to incorporate into itself something akin to minstrel culture. Whore's idea of developing enclaves contains the promise of a better future, one symbolized by the minstrels' remaining on stage as the curtain falls despite their failure to keep the IBMers from taking over the island.

The hope Whore's relationship offers may be what the musical most owes to Orwell's *Nineteen Eighty-Four* (1949)—beyond the IBM version of Newspeak called Federal Standardized English—the novel that Pynchon and Sale "vamped off" to develop their play (Gibbs 35). Such is the case if Pynchon recognized as early as 1958 the significance that he later attributes to the tense and nature of the English used in the essay, "The Principles of Newspeak," in the novel's appendix. "Newspeak," Pynchon writes, "was supposed to have become general by 2050, and yet it appears that it did not last long, let alone triumph, that the ancient humanistic ways of thinking inherent in standard English have persisted, survived, and ultimately prevailed, and that perhaps the social and moral order it speaks for has even, somehow, been restored" (xxiv). Whether or not the understanding of *Nineteen Eighty-Four*'s appendix that Pynchon articulates in 2003 dates back to the late fifties, "Minstrel Island" seems to be for Pynchon, as well as Sale, an attempt to conceive a way to escape ongoing oppressive conditions by drawing on Orwell's positing love as a subversive force, an attitude toward love that seems to have affinities with Pynchon's own at the time and since.[82] He told Mahool and Sale, for instance, that he was sorry not to have seen them before leaving Ithaca for New York City, explaining "i like to see young people together and happy"—a line that shows up as "I like to see young people get together" in "The Small Rain" and *V.* (48 and 24) and as "I do like t.s.y.p.g.t" in the letter in which he congratulates Kirk on his impending marriage to Faith (May 28, 1962)[83]—because "it seems to me that in these uncertain times the sight of a bright and charming couple sharing all the advantages of togetherness can almost restore ones faith in a just and merciful providence" (To Kirkpatrick Sale and Patricia Mahool c. January 1959).

II

Pynchon's attraction to enclaves in which dissent seems sustainable dates back at least to his senior year in high school, when he wrote, before he had reached sixteen, the fictional epistolary sequence the "Voice of the Hamster," along with "Ye Legend of Sir Stupid and the Purple Knight" and "The Boys," for his school newspaper, *Purple and Gold*. The pieces display not only Pynchon's interest in oppositional behavior but also his feel, just seven or eight years after he began writing (see Weisenburger 695), for the linguistic and social possibilities that fiction can offer. The Hamster High pieces, including "The Boys"—an account of an actual event—have interested previous critics only marginally, being read, if at all, for the ways they reflect concerns and techniques that Pynchon would work with as he developed into the writer he has become. If we look at the pieces for themselves, however, we discover more value in them than that which is produced by the retroactively determined interest that brings us to the material in the first place. Pynchon builds a fictional space and imagines its influence on the world beyond it, if we take five of the six articles as parts of a whole, the outlier in the scheme being the "Purple Knight," a story that, nonetheless, relates to the Hamster High sequence in one respect.

The voice in "Voice of the Hamster" is Boscoe Stein,[84] a student at Hamster High who writes letters to Sam, a student at Oyster Bay High. The name "Boscoe" can serve as an entrance into our reading of the work. Charles Hollander associates it with the "once-popular chocolate syrup" (46) Bosco, asserting that it is "Pynchon's earliest [*known*, it must be added,] 'feint,' a real thing, differing from the character's name by one letter," a reasonable assumption given that another Hamster High student is called Trodsky, a name surely meant to be associated with "Trotsky" to draw further attention to the nonconforming inclinations of Hamster High's community and, in doing so, to disassociate it's voice from the two powers at the heart of the cold war, the U.S., because Trotsky was a communist, and the U.S.S.R., because Stalin had condemned Trotsky, forced him into exile, and had him assassinated. The yell of Moe Klonk, whose name means "sounded tired" in Dutch, against "capitalistic oppression and bourgeois tyranny" can then be distanced, in the larger context of the sequence of articles, from Soviet-style leftist thinking, which the American Right sought to elide with leftist thought in general to cast it as unAmerican.

Klonk's name, if not the introduction of the character, is expertly employed, suggesting a jaded Klonk understands that his call for change will be misunderstood or ignored and repressed: he thus "got acquainted with the business end of a nightstick the hard way, and that sort of put an end to the party" (160–61), the pun intentional, one imagines.

Hollander goes on to note that Boscoe "is not sweet and syrupy, but acerbic and a bit nasty," and attributes Pynchon's failure to forge an association between the character and his name to artistic immaturity (Hollander 46). Perhaps Pynchon was making another association. "Bosco" is also Italian for "a wood"—a relevant connection to make in a story about a school founded by J. Fattington Woodgrouse, the name of a woodland chicken-like bird with the space between "wood" and "grouse" deleted—and suggests a cross-linguistic pun on "wood," making our correspondent a wooden stein, full of beer, one could add. Boscoe, after all, signs himself Sam's "drunken amigo" (158). He is an adolescent version of the wine-soaked Knight from "Ye Legend of Sir Stupid and the Purple Knight," who is similarly intent on wreaking havoc on his world. The play of associations does not end there. The Spanish call Hieronymus Bosch "El Bosco," something a member of the Spanish Club, as Pynchon was, might know, suggesting that we read the letters as a literary equivalent of *The Garden of Earthly Delights* (1503–1515). One notion informing the sequence seems to be that the stifling conditions on the rock off the South Shore where Hamster High is located have deadened the wood or garden, transforming it into a barren environment, and that Boscoe, along with his friends, is amplifying (through opposition) the remaining life, just as Bosco, the chocolate syrup—called a "Milk Amplifier" on the product's midcentury label—was said in the advertisements of the period to amplify milk's goodness as well as improve its desirability.[85] In the spirit of Romanticism, opposition to authority and cultural norms comes to represent the life force, and the crazy behavior of Hamster High's population can be regarded as life's prevailing over barrenness.

Such behavior is evident both among the adults and the students, although adult craziness is different, if not superficially so, from that of the students. The cast of adult characters includes the trigonometry teacher Mr. Faggiaducci, a former be-bop drummer who longs for his former life and uses, according to rumor, heroin; the principal Mr. Sowfurkle, a transplant from the Tennessee hills who still wields a shotgun and also plays the bagpipes, practicing during school hours, and whose name combines "sow," a female pig, and "furkle," a homonym of the German "ferkel," a piglet, syllables that Boscoe shortens to "Furk," thereby suggesting "fuck" and making Sowfurkle a female-piglet fucker; and Coach Willis, who drinks heavily and chain-smokes. These characters, derived from types—jazz musician, backwoodsman, and high-school and thus local coach—that were on the margins of mid-twentieth-century American culture, do not form a united opposition: they each stand alone, and their behavior is not part of a conscious effort at subversion but a symptomatic response to the conditions under which they exist, conditions the rock's isolation, or status as an enclave, aggravates. Hence Coach Willis, when the bad example of his drinking leads to his job being threatened, denies responsibility for his behavior, claiming "it's the teams that have driven him to drink" ("Juvenilia," 158). Moreover, when the school is checked for institutional compliance by the State Educational Inspector, the grandson of the school's founder, the adults illustrate their desire for conformity by "warmly" (158) welcoming, rather than resisting or offering duplicitous civilities to, the present-day Mr. Woodgrouse, who suffers comic and, for the most part, accidental punishments—much as Miss Phipps, the chemistry teacher, is punished when she intrudes upon Mr. Sowfurkle's "inner sanctum" (157). The surfacing of Hamster

High's symptoms of peculiarity leads to Woodgrouse's being repeatedly injured, as "always happens when somebody we don't want comes wandering around" (159), and finally causes him to suffer a mental breakdown.

The source of intentional opposition is the students, particularly the group whose members are called The Boys, although it may be singled out because Boscoe counts himself a member. The jocks, for instance, also indulge in oppositional behavior: the football players "consistently ru[n] the wrong way," the basketball players refuse "to dribble the ball," and those on the track team are "afraid to high jump, and [they] thro[w] the shot-put underhand" (158). The behavior would appear to be intentional, a concerted effort to torment Coach Willis. The track team's fear, however, may suggest that the athletes are not always capable of controlling their behavior. Indeed, the teams' playfulness is described to illustrate the oddness that the school's isolation is said to cause, that is, is among the details brought forth to give Sam a macrocosmic view of the Hamster High environment. The way the students' behavior is introduced implies that the reader is being asked to assume that it is not conscious activity. Still, the difference between an unconscious or a conscious source of the students' and faculty's conduct remains ambiguous. The difficulty such ambiguity creates is an issue elsewhere in the Hamster articles. The clearest instance of this difficulty is, in fact, resolved for the reader, if not for all the characters involved. Faggiaducci's feeling persecuted is diagnosed by his psychologist as his having the sort of delusions that Freud associated with latent homosexuality (see 29),[86] as his reacting to unconscious inclinations, but there really is a conspiracy against the teacher. Our perspective on the teams' playfulness could be, though isn't necessarily, analogous to the psychologist's perspective on Faggiaducci's apparent paranoia.

The group called The Boys is introduced in the third article (160–61), when Boscoe switches the perspective to a microcosmic view and focuses on Faggiaducci, who acquires a first name, Rafael, and the group takes on the role that the isolated environment is said in the first article to foster. The experiment to cause the "psychoanalytic deletion of the super-ego" (161) of Faggiaducci is analogous to the destruction of Inspector Woodgrouse, the super-ego in the individual functioning the way the overseer of state regulations should in the school or the way a teacher should do in a classroom, for that matter. Names again alert us to the group's symbolic significance, particularly those of its leaders, Big Bob Woods, who is named to establish an echo with the "wood" alluded to earlier, and the redheaded Crazy Harrigan, the more important figure in the sequence. The latter's name is taken from the title of a 1907 George M. Cohan song about the nineteenth-century performer and playwright Edward Harrigan, a song that Pynchon would likely have known from the Cohan biopic *Yankee Doodle Dandy* (1942), where it is anachronistically treated as a piece Cohan wrote while he was trying to establish himself and thus as material that played a part in bringing his career to life. The song's theme, pride in one's Irish heritage or outsider status, is a somewhat anomalous one in Cohan's body of work, which is most famous for its patriotic American slant. In fact, Cohan set out to create musicals that were truly American rather than dependent on European models, as were the shows appearing on the Broadway stage when he began writing; he succeeded, and is now "[c]onsidered the father of American musical comedy" (Rollins 250).

The name Harrigan links the Pynchon character to the figure of the alien, one capable of undermining a dominant model and fashioning a new one, that is, if Pynchon drew upon the connection between Harrigan's Irish pride and Cohan's, a pride *Yankee Doodle Dandy* ties to Cohan's early development as a writer and entertainer.[87] But even without the Cohan biography, the reader should treat Harrigan's name as signifying the transformative potential of his, as well as The Boys', function, if only because of its origin in a song. In the Hamster articles, music is a source of opposition and revival, regardless of genre: the examples include be-bop, bagpipe music, and pop. The last is represented, beyond the "Harrigan" allusion, by "High Noon," the song that opens the 1952 movie of the same name, a line from which, adapted for the Hamster High context, is sung as part of the Faggiaducci experiment, with Trodsky accompanying the performance on guitar (161), a detail that perhaps makes Trodsky the Pynchon figure in the piece, assuming Pynchon, who plays guitar or did so in his youth, was already using characters as partial surrogates.[88] The use to which music is put in the sequence also helps clarify the difference between adults' symptomatic response to stifling conditions and students' opposition. The adults turn to music without any intention other than finding relief from the demands of the day; the students employ it for oppositional purposes. Faggiaducci is an exception, or was when he was a professional be-bop drummer, but that was in the past, during the youth he relives playfully for his students. He might be described, in Boscoe's words, as "[a] real 'gone guy'" (157), that is, as "cool," but that guy is gone, having been left in a past that Faggiaducci now replays in a comic mode, for instance, by "telling be-bop jokes in class" (157).

While all the observed adult subversive behavior, including the teachers' engagement with music, can be defined as symptomatic reactions to confinement to the rock, student opposition (or young people's if we count the younger Faggiaducci's life as a drummer) is more widespread, leaking onto the mainland, notably among Sam's cohorts, "Beer-belly MacPherson and the rest of the mob" (158). Such leakage serves as an implicit commentary on the stifling conditions of 1950s American culture. To emphasize that implication, Pynchon turns to student rebellion outside the epistolary fiction and in the article "The Boys" writes directly about Oyster Bay High, where a group, inspired by "a certain series of articles in the P. & G." (166) and calling itself "The Boys" (167), comes together in the cause of "goofing off" (166) and around a mutual love of math. Initially known only to "their own compact enclave" (167), The Boys emerge into officialdom when they gather for a yearbook picture. Mr. X., the school's own be-bop-influenced math teacher, is not, at first, joining the group for the photo, but The Boys coax him into the collective with the cry "We want X!" This action is reminiscent, if only vaguely so, of the fictional Boys' pushing Faggiaducci into insanity by singing the adapted line from "High Noon," "Do not forsake me, Faggiaducci." Seriousness to frivolity is the trajectory in both cases. Mr. X, however, comes down to The Boys and begins "a new era of student-teacher relations" (167). If only at this one point, Pynchon's juvenilia "exude an optimism rarely found in his professional fiction" (Hartnett), at least prior to *Vineland*. It is a moment, ostensibly outside the pages of a fiction, in which student rebelliousness and teacherly authority unite in communal understanding and celebration.

III

Epistolary fiction incorporates Oyster Bay High's culture, elements of which are drawn into the narrative, while its culture incorporates the fiction, the power of which is transformative. Analogously, material in Pynchon's letters, a metonym for biography here, contextualizes his work and is contextualized by it—as the above discussion of Pynchon's use of Ginsberg's "negro streets" discloses. The letters then serve, in one of their functions, as framing devices, something

David Foster Wallace suggests, if indirectly, when he builds part of *Infinite Jest*'s (1996) frame with an allusion to the letter Pynchon sent to the *New York Times* in response to Romain Gary's accusation that he had stolen the name Genghis Cohen. Pynchon described Gary's problem as "perhaps more psychiatric than literary" ("Pros and Cohns" 24), a sentiment Wallace echoes when he claims that any resemblance between one of his characters and an actual person is the product of coincidence or "your own troubled imagination" (viii). Framing separates interpreters from the object and often clarifies their perception of it,[89] an idea evidently confirmed by the fact that of the two available Pynchon novel manuscripts, only the one that became *V.*, the one that a reading of which can be framed by letters, has been discussed. The *Vineland* manuscript sits unexplored, the story behind its transformation either lost or yet to emerge.

The extant letters surrounding the preparation of *V.* for publication and its aftermath, both those between Pynchon and Corlies Smith and those to Faith Sale, do more than help us frame the process through which the novel emerged out of the manuscript. They also add nuance to our understanding of Pynchon, allowing some insight into the "compact enclave" of his private self and the relation that Pynchon aims to construct between that enclave and the world beyond it. The correspondence, for example, undercuts the view that Pynchon was some kind of independent genius from the beginning and illustrates his discomfort with being thought of in such terms. That notion was promoted by the marketing department at Lippincott when it called *V.* "the most important piece of fiction written since ULYSSES" (*V.* [ARC] cover blurb) and later by Smith, who said he suggested Pynchon make "a half-dozen minor changes [to *V.*]; Pynchon, 'extremely reasonable,' listened and agreed to three" (Dudar 36). The latter statement makes it sound as if the difference between the manuscript and the book were slight. Smith made three suggestions, one of them major, that is, the removal of Sphere from the narrative; Pynchon countered with fourteen, and Smith commented upon those (see Smith to P, February 23, 1962, and March 20, 1962; P to Smith, March 13, 1962). This summary still conceals the work that went into redrafting the manuscript, work for which Pynchon did not take full credit, assuring Faith that without her, Smith, and Catherine Carver (the copy editor who also came up with the title), the book wouldn't be nearly as good as it is, while blaming himself for failures he perceived (To Faith Sale, October 1, 1962; To Kirkpatrick and Faith Sale, March 9, 1963).

Whenever Pynchon discusses his own writing, he becomes a critic, manifesting his inclination to admire a more classical ideal or academic view of literature. Hence he tells the Sales that "the only kind of novel that is worth a shit" is "the traditional realistic kind," adding that such a novel is "what, someday, I would like to be able to write" (June 29, 1963). Pynchon also hinted at the classical component of his approach to his work when he told David Hajdu about Fariña's opposition to critical authority in college. Any time someone became critic-like, "there would always be Dick, pointing his finger, laughing, yelling, 'Critic!' 'Who,' you would say, 'me? Not me, man.' 'Eclectic,' he would yell back, 'academic, pedant. Ha!' He'd be right, of course. It helped keep you straight. [. . .] He was like a conscience" (Hajdu 46). For Pynchon, that conscience came to serve more as an external than as an internal guide. It would take him a while to embrace it at all. As late as 1963, the last time he looked at Fariña's novel before it was in proofs, Pynchon ignored the Fariña-esque conscience, assuming the moment warranted a critic to help improve the work. Fariña wanted praise, not advice, and Pynchon apologizes once the book is nearing publication, offering unqualified approval: "Did my reaction in Carmel seem less enthusiastic? I was being analytical then. Because you had asked me to. And there is that bit of the nasty/analytical to us all, right? [...] If you want complaints, sorry, I don't have any" (October 16, 1965).

If someone praised one of Pynchon's novels the way Pynchon praised Fariña's *Been Down So Long*, he would never take it seriously. Indeed, he advises a young aspiring novelist who reached out to him for advice in the late seventies, "if you are truly interested in *not* kissing ass, don't write to writers you don't know and tell them 'I can't read novels with much interest anymore. . . . The only ones I can read are yours.' Besides being impossible to believe, it makes the whole thing read like a form letter" (To a Young Novelist, May 21, 1978), that is, bereft of spirit or genuine critical analysis. Despite what he told Fariña, "nasty" isn't an adjective that Pynchon ordinarily conflates with "analytical," and he seems to have done so while writing to Fariña only to appeal to Fariña's sensibility. Pynchon values having errors pointed out and receiving criticism that adds to his knowledge of his work and self. He thus calls Carver's copy editing a helpful diagnostic; notes he has saved reviews and "personal reactions" of friends so that he might, "in a year or so [...], study them to see what went wrong with *V.*"; and accepts Kirk's or Faith's critique of that novel's "lack of suspense" (see To Faith Sale, October 1, 1962; To Faith and Kirkpatrick Sale, June 2, 1963; To Kirkpatrick and Faith Sale, June 29, 1963). More tellingly, he thanks Stanly Hyman for his review, which Pynchon observes "made me aware of things about the book and about myself I had not been aware of but which happen to be true, and which I have since for better or worse had to make allowances for. That kind of feedback, being honest, is valuable, and rare, and I appreciate it" (December 8, 1965). His thinking about uncritical praise seems to be summed up in his letter to Shetzline and Beal, when he wrote, "give me a break from these stories [about] how great I am. [...] I can't handle it [. . .], and besides you know deep down that it's applesauce" (January 21, 1974).[91]

The response to the praise Shetzline and Beal were passing on to him was made in the wake of the publication of *Gravity's Rainbow*, the book that gave Pynchon the confidence to accept he got it right once, or was a "one-shot flash-in-the-pan amateur" (To Barthelme), the publications before 1973 representing practice, apprenticeship and journeyman work as he calls it in the *Slow Learner* introduction. The letters, at least occasionally, also clearly serve as practice: he tries out lines that show up later in his published work and exchanges with the Sales feghoots, a genre that originally featured the character Ferdinand Feghoot—who appears in the examples Pynchon sends to the Sales—and that concludes in an elaborate pun. Pynchon employs the genre in his novels, most notoriously in *Gravity's Rainbow* when he develops a long digression to set up the line "For De Mille, young fur-henchman can't be rowing" (559), a pun on the phrase "Forty million Frenchmen can't be wrong" (see Weisenburger, *Companion* 292 for a discussion of the pun). Pynchon was constitutionally drawn to the genre, it would seem, for before the first Ferdinand Feghoot stories were published in 1956, he had played, at least once, with the technique of building up a story to lead into an elaborate pun. The revelation about the origin of the Purple Knight in "Ye Legend of Sir Stupid and the Purple Knight" is accompanied by King Arthur's exclaiming, "I say, Old Fotheringay's gone and fallen into the wine vat! Old Fotheringay! Haw, Haw, Haw! Old Fotheringay's got high on grape juice! Haw! In the still of the knight!" (166).

The implied contrast that emerges in Pynchon's letters between Pynchon's and Fariña's views of their own writing—

on the one hand, a trial from which to gain insight, or something to use to test possibilities, and on the other hand, a finished product to be taken for what it is and consumed—suggests an inside/outside dynamic in Pynchon's thought that inverts, in a sense, the one that offers hope for the soon-to-be dispossessed occupiers of Camelot in "Minstrel Island," as well as for the musical's assumed audience. If the ending of "Minstrel Island" was to imply that the minstrels would carry on their resistance by fashioning individual, internal beatnik paradises, Pynchon's biography suggests that his own personal mode of resistance to America's cultural flatland (to use *Inherent Vice*'s nomenclature) as well as to conventional or easily appropriated elements of the alternatives, was to fashion something akin to a rational manipulator within, a contrast suggested by Pynchon's understanding of the difference between himself and Fariña. Fariña "was the crazy one, I was the rationalist—he was *engagé*, I was reserved—he was relaxed, I was stuffy" (43), Pynchon explained to Hajdu.

In effect, Pynchon comes to reside in his works as something akin to Maxwell's Demon in the Nefastis Machine: a rational being capable of resisting homogenization. He suggests as much in a letter to Arthur Mizener, a professor he studied with at Cornell. "[T]he further I get into this wretched profession the clearer it is that I am doing very little consciously beyond some clerk routine—assembling, expediting—and that either (a) there is an Extra-personal Source, or (b) readers are the ones who do most of the work, or all of the above. Which is not at all a bring down to realize. Just the opposite." The gifted reader is the "sensitive," to use John Nefastis's terminology (see *CL49* 104–06), while the Extra-personal Source is perhaps some kind of "paranormal process," as Weisenburger understands the statement ("Gravity's Rainbow" 44), or is the moment in cultural history that Pynchon occupies and the place in the social body from which his work derives, to speak more secularly and suggest a more sane third term than the portrait of Clerk Maxwell, which Nefastis regards as a conduit for a paranormal process in his machine but whose subject Oedipa sees as a physical body with a round forehead and curly hair; then as a psychological being with "hangups, crises, spookings in the middle of the night" (106); and finally as an unknowable inhabitant of his time who "gazed into some vista of Victorian England" (107).

Staring at the image of Maxwell does not lead to communication between Oedipa and the Demon; the piston remains unmoved. The whole episode could be read, in part, as a critique of the lionization, or perhaps a better word would be apotheosis, of the author, particularly through a focus on or obsession with his/her image. Such focus fails to provide readers access to the power of the text. The notion that communication, both metaphorical and actual, is of value in warding off entropy is nonetheless to be taken seriously in Pynchon's fiction, particularly in "Entropy," the short story that explores in a social setting the concepts that consume Nefastis. Thermodynamic entropy isn't left out of the story: its importance is established, albeit in explicitly "social terms," in Callisto's part of it. Callisto saw "in American 'consumerism' [...] a [...] tendency from the least to the most probable, from differentiation to sameness, from ordered individuality to a kind of chaos. He found himself, in short, restating [J. Willard] Gibbs' prediction in social terms, and envisioned a heat-death for his culture in which ideas, like heat energy, would no longer be transferred" (91). There is, however, no Demon like the one that Nefastis posits as controlling his machine and "mak[ing] the metaphor not only verbally graceful, but also objectively true" (*CL49* 106). Rather, obsession with the metaphor, in Callisto's case, turns it into a delusion, while the concept becomes, for Meatball

Mulligan, a useful tool, employed unwittingly, to stave off entropy in his environment. Callisto and Meatball become, in effect, the Demons in their respective systems, one whose power is failing and one whose power gets discovered.

Despite Callisto's intention in establishing a "hermetically sealed [...] enclave of regularity" (83), his influence is entropic, cutting off, as much as is possible, the transfer of heat/information to and from the outside, that is, to and from the collection of other enclaves—which we might loosely think of as molecules, that is, as individual units that together make up the whole—in "the city's chaos" (83), enclaves that are, Callisto believes, more or less indistinguishable from each other. The relationship between Callisto's apartment and the city is something like the relationship between the small bird that Callisto holds and Callisto himself, an analogy that gains strength if we take into account the lifespan of the bird, likely a bluebird, the eastern variety of which can live up to seven years (see Terres 94), the same amount of time Callisto has spent creating his hothouse apartment (see *SL* 83). The healthy bird, in short, represents a functioning system that Callisto has sustained, but it is now sick and will soon be dead, an inevitability that Callisto seeks to frustrate by transferring heat from his body to its. However, as Luc Herman notes, "since a bird's average body temperature is higher than a human being's, Callisto inadvertently takes heat away from the animal instead of furnishing it" (22), quickening its demise. Similarly, Callisto's apartment is a system, a "hothouse jungle" (83), that has its needs delivered from the outside (84) but that cannot last forever. After Aubade smashes out the window, the higher temperature within the apartment is taken out of it, and it loses, more quickly than would have been the case if the window were left intact, its status as an enclave: the environment, in short, begins to be reabsorbed into the city.

Meatball's apartment, like Callisto's, serves as a sort of enclave but of a superficially different nature, at least at the moment. Callisto strives toward enclosed perfection, while Meatball fosters and celebrates transition. His party has come together to mark a lease-breaking, a liminal moment between residences. It's ending will signal having to settle down into a sort of stasis, something the party avoids by reaching new transitional moments, moving from "gathering its second wind" (82) at the story's beginning to "trembl[ing] on the threshold of its third day" (97) near its end. Between these two moments, the party risks succumbing to entropy and ending prematurely. As the party is progressing, those in the apartment are becoming isolated, either as unrelated groups—in the guise of Sandor Rojas and his three friends at the story's very beginning, of the Duke di Angelis quartet, of the sailors when they arrive, and of the shouting *morra* players near the story's end—or as lone individuals—the girl Meatball moves from the sink to the shower being the clearest example—that do not communicate with each other, although they all interact with Meatball. The party thus moves toward a rupture comparable to that which leads to the dissolution of Saul's marriage, that is, if we view the party as a collection of individuals and/or groups in a supposed-to-be parallel connected circuit—with the individuals or groups functioning like bulbs attached in a string of lights that allows any that remain connected to it to continue shining even if others are disconnected—drawing on Saul, who describes communication between two people in a relationship as "a closed circuit" (90) that can be disrupted by "Ambiguity. Redundancy. Irrelevance, even. Leakage. All this is noise. Noise screws up your signal, makes for disorganization in the circuit" (90–91).

The "noise" that disrupts Saul's "circuit" is the ambiguity of the word "love," and it is the problems surrounding the search for love or the playing with it that bring disorganization to the party, thereby illustrating the inverse of Callisto's realization that love "not only makes the world go round but also makes the boccie ball spin, the nebula process" (84–85). Love's power is problematic: it is a force of life and togetherness as well as a force of separation and death, the latter of which Pynchon admits associating with sex during the period in which he was writing his short stories (*SL* 5). Such ambiguity is also present in the 37° temperature, which is cold on the Fahrenheit scale but the temperature of the human body, or warm, on the Celsius scale. The sailors—who arrive in the belief that the apartment is a whorehouse and ignore Meatball's denials in a conversation that illustrates a broken circuit—are, after all, looking for love in one of its senses, the sense referred to in the song "Love for Sale," the inspiration for the musical experiment that gives us a view of entropy from a different perspective.

The Duke di Angelis quartet takes the experiment of "Love for Sale," that is, its elimination of "root chords" so that one is obliged to think "the roots," and transforms it into an experiment in which one is obliged "to think everything. [. . .] Roots, line, everything" (95). Noise seems to be eliminated but is, paradoxically, increased. Not only does each musician need to think everything, but each audience member also needs to do so, while observing ambiguous signals: for example, "Vincent began to fling his arms around, his fists clenched; then, abruptly, was still, then repeated the performance" (94). The likely result is a different thought not just in each listener's head but in each performer's as well and a collection of different, if internal, sounds that are not communicated to anyone, something externally represented by "[t]he noise in Meatball's apartment" reaching "a sustained ungodly crescendo" (96). That crescendo begins after a "government girl in a Bennington sweatshirt" arrives to keep her love secure. She was "recently engaged to an ensign attached to the Forrestal," the sailors' ship, and "came charging into the kitchen, head lowered, and butted Slab in the stomach" (96), presumably to encourage Slab, the seaman apprentice who seems to be leading his shipmates, to stop negatively influencing her fiancé.

Observing that his party is "deteriorating into total chaos," Meatball figures that he can deal with the problem in either of two ways: "(a) lock himself in a closet and maybe eventually they would go away, or (b) try to calm everybody down, one by one" (96). Option a "repeats on a smaller scale," as David Seed puts it, "Callisto's retreat into a hot-house" (46). The possibility that partygoers would kick down the closet door, unseal the space, would be analogous to Aubade's breaking the window. Meatball's surmising that the uninvited sailors, the "crew off the good ship Lollipop or whatever it was" (97), would unseal the closet emphasizes that the noise they bring to the party has served to quicken its present deterioration. Emerging from the closet, Meatball would find that little had changed, and he would be swept back into the chaos that he sought to escape. He thus begins to reintroduce a working order to the proceedings, reconnecting, so to say, the "bulbs" to the current of the party—resupplying the sailors with wine, separating the *morra* players to silence the noise they are producing, introducing Sandor Rojas to the government girl to keep her out of trouble, moving the girl out of the shower, and talking with Saul—and the party is revived. Emphasizing the significance of Meatball's actions, Pynchon also has Meatball call a repairman to fix the refrigerator so that its connection to the apartment's current can again be made functional.

The reference to the sailors in Meatball's closet-fantasy suggests something else. It suggests a relationship between the closet and Meatball's own apartment. The crew upends the peace that the party had been settling into, just as Meatball imagines it disrupting his further retreat. The sailors, nonetheless, embody the spirit of the party, serving the same function in a party about to quiet down as the breaking of a lease serves in an apartment that has ceased to enable kicks, a problem that Meatball's response to "Tea time" (*SL* 85) illustrates, but that spirit needs to be channeled to keep its potentially destructive nature in check. Meatball's decision to engage the partygoers can thus be viewed as a model not just for stopping the decent into chaos but also for avoiding an acceptance of stasis in a new residence once the old lease is broken. The story's turning back to Callisto's apartment at the point at which Meatball engages the partygoers may serve not as a fatalistic reminder that entropy is inevitable but as a warning against identifying Callisto's life as some sort of heroic resistance and against seeing in it "the romantic glamour associated with a defiant withdrawal into a self-constructed space," as Simon Malpas and Andrew Taylor would have us view Option a (38). Callisto's refusal to engage the world ensures his virtual demise. Concluding in Callisto's apartment, moreover, has the effect of leaving Meatball's party at story's end suspended in an indefinite state of continuance.

Kasia Boddy, discussing the choices Pynchon had to make as a writer, asserts that Pynchon faced the same dilemma as Meatball—either retreating, Callisto-like, from the world or engaging with it—and made the choice analogous to the one Meatball makes: "The 'academic enclosure' and stasis of the short story[, analogous, for Boddy, to Meatball's closet,] proved too stuffy for him" (57). The choice between "academic enclosure" (*SL* 22) and the outside was also the choice, a less metaphorical one, before Pynchon when he was offered the Wilson Fellowship that would have kept him, if he hadn't turned it down, at the university, teaching and pursuing graduate studies. Pynchon, of course, never overcame his desire to maintain an enclave of privacy, but he learned not to confine himself to that enclave, a lesson his relationship with Fariña seems to have taught him. After Fariña's death, Pynchon wrote Mimi Baez-Fariña that he owed his late friend more than he could say, "both personal and writerly" (quoted in Hajdu 178). The debt reveals itself not in an internalization of Fariña's approach to life and work but in Pynchon's coming to accept that his inclination to remain reserved could be put aside, at least partially—certainly by way of publication, but also by going out and listening "to the American voices around" him (*SL* 22)—and that things, if not what those things taught, could be let go. He thus acquiesces to a request from Mizener to reprint "Entropy," even though he notes, "I was and still am ashamed I ever wrote the thing." After attempting to explain its flaws, explanations omitted from the letter, he realized that "an ego trip," the critical voice's warning him to hold himself back, was dictating his response and that the external voice—the discourse produced when the voices of the text and of its readers join—has value beyond the author's isolated one.

Epilogue

NEAR the beginning of the present study, while discussing the notion that there are two Pynchons, Tom Pynchon the private individual and Thomas Pynchon the public, if hidden, figure that his readers imagine, I hypothesize that the U.S. marketing campaign for *Bleeding Edge* highlighted the divide between these two Pynchons. I note that the campaign—the releasing of a book trailer that features the twenty-something Sleazus wearing a t-shirt that reads "Hi, I'm Tom Pynchon" and the posting of images on social media of miscellaneous people wearing a promotional t-shirt that reads "Hi I'm Thomas Pynchon"—calls attention to how readers' fiction-making impulses influence their construction of the notion of both the private and the public Pynchon. Penguin Press's book trailer was followed by another one produced for the German publisher Rowohlt that seems, I also note, to contain at least one allusion to the U.S. promotional campaign. Although the German trailer uses a more realistic, because elderly, Pynchon character, it also undermines a realistic reading of the author-appearance by drawing the scene and the figure who walks through it into Pynchon's fiction through allusions to and citations from it, particularly to and from "Entropy."

Allusions to "Entropy" in the Rowohlt book trailer, I now want to propose, are also allusions to an inspiration for part of the U.S. marketing campaign, for that campaign also drew, if obliquely, on "Entropy," particularly for its dissemination of images of people wearing the Hi-I'm-Thomas-Pynchon t-shirt. The relationship between the face above each of those shirts and the author that each shirt proclaims its wearer to be—a symbol of the possibility that there might be as many ideas of Pynchon as there are people who imagine him—mirrors the relationship between the song the Duke di Angelis quartet performs and the song that must be thought by each member of its audience.

In the story, that unhearable song is tantamount to noise as understood in Saul's account of communication theory, an equivalence that strengthens the story's version of the connection it posits between communication and thermodynamic entropy: universal heat-death, after all, would exist in silence. The appropriation of the trope to characterize the relationship between the idea of Pynchon and his readers alters its import, for in the context of that relationship, the trope suggests that Pynchon's silence is a centropic force,[93] enabling his readers to negate entropy's ability to undermine community and bringing them together around a group of texts. These texts provide data that can be sorted, to draw on Nefastis's discussion of Maxwell's Demon, and transmitted, while the multiplicity of interpretive possibilities prevents a stagnant uniformity from draining life from the activity. The value of Pynchon's personal silence, analogous to the musical silence of the Duke di Angelis quartet, is therefore transformed into a life-affirming force.

Endnotes

1   Paul Royster's description of "Hallowe'en? Over Already?" as "a 500-word article on [Pynchon's] son's school Halloween picnic," information from the rare-bookseller Ken Lopez's Catalogue 135 or 139, is inaccurate. The picnic, mentioned at the beginning of the introductory paragraph, is only touched upon briefly and does not appear to have had anything to do with Hallowe'en, which had yet to arrive, suggesting the essay was written in mid-October. The picnic could have been as early as September, relating perhaps to the beginning of the school year. The Blessing of the Animals, mentioned right after the picnic, is held the first Sunday of October each year, and the trip to the Tenafly Nature Center took place, and is discussed, after the Blessing. The sequence suggests a progression of events from picnic, to missed Blessing, to field trip, and the "Over Already" of the title must therefore reference the date not of composition but of publication, January 1999, adding a note of disappointment to the essay, maybe because the second tour of the Cathedral did not take place.

2   The elephant had been a fixture of the Blessing for years; it was missing in 2011, "the elephant that normally came ha[ving] died" (Paz).

3   "Entropy" appeared in the *Best American Short Stories* in 1961; "Mortality and Mercy in Vienna," while it never appeared in the *Best American Short Stories*, did receive an honorable mention in that publication in 1960, an honor "Under the Rose" also received in 1962.

4   Diebold and Goodwin's assertion regarding Pynchon's lingering reputation seems to be corroborated in a review of *New World Writing 16* by Edwin Ochester in the *Cornell Daily Sun*, which notes that almost all the pieces in the collection are "handled with a certain integrity not always found in writers whose integrity is measured by their hirsuteness." The use of "hirsuteness" here is an allusion to the stereotype of the bearded beatnik intellectual, an allusion Ochester picks up in the next paragraph, when he writes that Pynchon "has a beard, of course, but he wears his for aesthetic and not professional reasons" (4). (For the use of "beard" as slang for beatnik intellectual, see Green 83.) Siegel confirms that Pynchon wore a beard, at least in 1958, a goatee according to Kirkpatrick Sale (Kachka 50), a fact that does not detract

from Ochester's metaphorical use of Pynchon's hirsuteness, Ochester's bringing up of which evinces continued discussion of Pynchon at Cornell after his departure, even before *V.* made him famous.

Ochester, besides satirizing a tendency to respect writers for their participation in a movement rather than for their work, also seems to be assuming his audience's knowledge not only of Pynchon's lingering reputation on campus as a sort of beatnik character but also of Pynchon's talent. He goes on to note, "Pynchon's new story, 'Lowlands' [*sic*], is probably the story most people in the Ithaca region would turn to first," though he observes, despite it's being "a very imaginative story. And really a very well written one [. . .] a display case for Pynchon's characteristic fine imagery and wit," "it is not the best Pynchon" (4). This last comment, while perhaps simply a comparison of "Low-lands" (1960) with the two stories that Pynchon had published the year before (the availability of which the review mentions), may suggest a wider knowledge of work Pynchon had written while a student.

    5   Batchelor later acknowledged that Salinger was not Pynchon (see Alexander 254–56). Coincidentally, Batchelor's son attended the Cathedral School at the same time as Pynchon's son, and an essay by Batchelor appears next to the latter part of "Hallowe'en? Over Already?" on page 3 of the January 1999 *Cathedral School Newsletter*.

    6   Brolin isn't entirely credible. He, for instance, told *MoviesAddicts.com*, in a discussion of his last scene in the movie, "All I was supposed to do is grab a joint, eat the joint, but then I saw the pot, (laughs) or Bigfoot saw the pot" ("Josh Brolin Interview, *Inherent Vice*"), suggesting it was his idea to devour Doc's entire stash, but the script says, "BIGFOOT starts to EAT DOC'S WEED BAG AND JOINTS. HE SWALLOWS ... BIGFOOT takes another BIG BITE OF DOC'S DRUGS ... FINDS SOME PILLS, EATS THEM UP, TOO" (125). The pills are absent in the filmed scene, meaning Bigfoot consumed only the pot, which is, unlike pills, clearly a hippie drug, and thus seems to take less drugs than were mentioned in the screenplay.

    7   That Pynchon is or was a coffee drinker seems a safe conjecture. Chrissie Wexler, in her contribution to the Pynchon List that was published by Jules Siegel in *Lineland*, recalls a collection of "four hundred coffee cans" (53) in Pynchon's apartment in Manhattan Beach in the late sixties, a detail also alluded to by Siegel in his famous *Playboy* article, "Who Is Thomas Pynchon ... And Why Did He Take Off With My Wife?," where he notes the brand was Hills Brothers (rpt. in *Lineland* where the title is given as "Who is Thomas

Pynchon . . . And Why Is He Taking Off With My Wife" 91. All references to Siegel's *Playboy* article are to the *Lineland* reprint.)

8   Lane says in late September or October; I take the date from *The Warren Commission Report* (323).

9   Tharaldsen told Kachka that Pynchon went to Seattle following her and her then-husband David Seidler's encouragement (see 50–51) and that she, who was working at Boeing, got him the job writing for *Bomarc Service News* (BSN) after he arrived. The memory seems to contradict in some ways what was already known about Pynchon's move. Sources point to the fact that Pynchon had told people he was leaving New York to work for Boeing. Donadio told Smith that Pynchon needed the advance on the novel he was working on to get to Seattle to start a job (see Dudar 36), and Pynchon told Sale's colleagues at the *New Leader* that "he was going to Seattle to work on the Boeing Aircraft Corporation's house organ" ("Between Issues" 2). Tharaldsen may simply have misremembered events. Pynchon could very well have gone out to Seattle sometime in 1959, say in October or November, being depressed, as she remembers, maybe about his breakup with Lillian Laufgraben, the young Jewish woman whose parents objected to her being involved with someone who wasn't Jewish (Portinari), and Tharaldsen could have gotten him an interview that led to his being offered the position, perhaps after he had returned to New York. The BSN articles from January and February 1960 that Adrian Wisnicki identifies in an endnote as possibly by Pynchon, that is, articles that must have been completed before "Pynchon's reported time at Boeing" (33n20) but that have stylistic affinities with articles Wisnicki identifies as Pynchon's, could have been writing samples, the product of assignments meant to confirm Pynchon's ability to do the job, for which companies sometimes ask and for which they sometimes provide research packages. Companies retain the right to use such work, whether or not the applicant is given or accepts the job. Sometimes s/he gets paid for the work. If the article published in January and the one published in February were Pynchon's, they must have been turned in sometime at the end of 1959. Whatever the details may be, Pynchon seems to have remained in New York until the end of January, when he signed the contract with Lippincott for *V.*

10   Smith was in Cleveland at an American Library Association convention, which took place between July 9 and July 15, 1961, and met Patricia Mahool, who had "typed most of Tom's manuscript" (Mahool, private correspondence). Mahool was among Pynchon's friends at Cornell and was Sale's girlfriend before Sale dated

Faith, as is evidenced by the earliest-written letter at the Harry Ransom Center, the only letter there that dates from Pynchon's Cornell days. The top of the first extant page reads "Mahool!. . .," which either ends a paragraph begun on the previous page or serves, as Krafft reads the text, as the salutation, the ellipsis standing in for Sale (private correspondence). A Post Script reads, in part, "hey kirk, dont get pissed off because I addressed this to you and only included pattys name in the salutation. [. . .]" Without knowing more about the context in which the letter was written, figuring out whether it is incomplete or not rests on one's understanding of "only included pattys name," which could mean that the name was placed, along with Sale's, in the salutation but not on the envelope or that it was the only name used in the salutation despite the letter's being addressed to Sale (c. January 1959). Mahool doesn't remember anything about the letter but says that Pynchon "always addressed [her] as Mahool" (private correspondence).

In Cleveland, Smith and Mahool discussed the typescript, and Smith told her a good title might be "The Yo-Yo World of Benny Profane." Pynchon must have learned about that conversation in July, disapproved of the suggested title, and told Donadio, who must have informed Smith, for the second paragraph of Smith's August 2, 1961, letter to Pynchon begins, "I saw Pat Mahool in Cleveland, and it is doubtless from her that you got the title THE YO-YO WORLD OF BENNY PROFANE. I guess Pat (or whoever) didn't make clear that this was simply a title that came to mind long before I had even finished the script." In an interview with Smith, Stephen Tomaske asked him if he remembered Mahool, whom Smith could not clearly recall, but he noted that he had only been in Cleveland once, for the American Library Association convention (Interview with Corlies M. Smith, August 3, 2001). Mahool, who also worked in the publishing industry during the first half of the 1960s, agrees that the meeting must have taken place at the convention (private correspondence).

11   The first address corresponds to the address in the page from the Seattle phone book reprinted on the first page of *Of a Fond Ghoul*, and the second to the one on the second page, which is also the address used by Pynchon after August 1961, when he was writing to Smith as well as Faith and Kirkpatrick Sale, at least until he left Seattle in October or November of 1962 after finishing his review of *V.*'s galleys; Pynchon uses the address on a letter written to Kirkpatrick on May 28, 1962, and one written to Faith about *V.* on October 1, 1962. The

next letter, dated November 23, 1962, is from Mexico. (For an account of the changes made to the galleys, see Herman, Krafft, and Krafft.)

12   Herman and Krafft, in "Fast Learner," note that Smith recalls, "since the decision [to accept the novel] had to be cleared with his boss, he must have received the novel perhaps three or four weeks before the beginning of August" (2), when he wrote Pynchon the note. Smith had forgotten that the novel had been accepted by July 10, but given the need to have three or four weeks for the boss's approval, Lippincott must have gotten the typescript much earlier than Smith remembered. We may never learn whether Donadio received a note, as the Pynchon correspondence with her that will eventually become available at the Morgan Library begins in March 1963 (see Gussow).

At least two sources suggest that the typescript was not mailed to Donadio. Robert Goolrick, in "Pieces of Pynchon," writes, discussing his trepidation about contacting Donadio when he set out to find Pynchon in 1978, "[A]s it turns out, she loves to talk about Thomas Pynchon, who walked into her office, aged 24, with the manuscript of *V.* in his hand." In an interview with Tomaske, Harriet Wasserman, Donadio's secretary for a short period at Herb Jaffe in the 1950s and her assistant during part of the 1960s, claimed to remember the episode. "I was sitting in the waiting area where her desk was. She had just recently come to Russell & Volkening. I saw a guy come in with a fedora hat and a belted trench coat, and a box and a mustache. And when he left, she said, 'I just had a call from an editor at *Dial* [James Silberman] who said, "I'm going to send someone over to you. He's either insane or he's a genius."' And when he left, she said, 'That was the guy.' And it was Thomas Pynchon and it was *V.*" (Tomaske, Interview with Harriet Wasserman, June 28, 2001).

Wasserman's story and the account Donadio gave Goolrick lack credibility. Donadio had been representing Pynchon for some time before the typescript of *V.* was completed, having negotiated the contract before receiving the novel. The novel typescript still could have been hand delivered to Donadio's office. Given the fact that Mahool was working for St. Martin's Press when she typed the manuscript, it is possible that Pynchon mailed his draft to friends in New York and that after it was retyped, it was delivered to Donadio in the package in which it had arrived, hence her remembering years later that Pynchon had personally delivered the typescript, which he would do when he finished *Gravity's Rainbow*. (For the account of Pynchon's delivering *Gravity's Rainbow*, see McLellan.) In any case, once Mahool finished typing the manuscript, it had to be either given directly to Donadio or mailed back to Pynchon for proofing before being sent back to New York.

Wasserman could also have mixed up events. Her account of Pynchon's acquiring Donadio as an agent complements what we know about the event in other respects. Herbert Gold was at Cornell in Pynchon's final year—having taken over the position Vladimir Nabokov had held—and had get-togethers at his home with students, Pynchon and Fariña among them. Gold was impressed enough by Pynchon and Fariña to put them in contact with Silberman, who reminisced in a letter to Pynchon after Fariña's death, "When Herb Gold was at Cornell in '59, was it, he put me onto two writers—you and Dick. What a long time ago" (To Pynchon, July 5, 1966). Silberman later told John Calvin Batchelor, for "The Ghost of Richard Fariña," "Yes. I'd met [Fariña] years before, when I was with Dial Press. He and his friend, Tom Pynchon, had come down from Cornell, trying to get their stories in the *Dial* magazine" (26). Silberman did not think the stories of either were suitable for *Dial* but saw potential in Pynchon, sending him to Donadio, who was impressed enough with what she read to take Pynchon on as a client either before his graduation from Cornell or in the weeks following it.

Another problem with Wasserman's account is that Donadio apparently had not yet begun to work for Russell & Volkening when she received the typescript, a point raised by the July 10 internal Lippincott memo's discussion of paying Pynchon the monies Lippincott owed him on the advance—that is, the $1,000 that he was to get upon his delivery and Lippincott's acceptance of the novel. The memo reveals that Lippincott would not pay Pynchon the money until some concerns over legal issues had been resolved. Donadio had been working for Herb Jaffe Associates in January 1960, when the contract was signed and Pynchon was paid $500, but by the time *V.* reached Lippincott, Herb Jaffe had sold his agency to Ashley-Steiner. The contract, it was at least believed, had not been automatically transferred to the latter agency, and in order for any payment to be made, the memo says, Jaffe and Pynchon would need to sign a "paper" transferring the contract to Ashley-Steiner, where Donadio must have remained for a while before moving to Russell & Volkening. That issue was quickly settled, probably without Pynchon's participation, for a hand-written addendum dated July 17 underneath the body of the memo text notes that the check had been mailed, likely to Donadio.

13   There were two addresses: 4217 11th Street, N.E., Seattle and 4212 Pasadena, Seattle. The conjecture that they may have been mailing addresses is Krafft's (private correspondence). The fact that mail sent to the first is sent "c/o Seidler" adds strength to the conjecture, though Pynchon may have received mail at 11th Street only while he was staying with David Seidler and looking for his own place. The prefatory phrase in the memo also suggests that those at Lippincott thought Pynchon might be having mail sent to a friend's place.

14   In a letter dated November 10, 1960, Smith thanks Pynchon for meeting him.

15   Smith did not read Pynchon as unapproachable, noting in his first letter about the typescript that "it needs some work" (August 2, 1961) and promising specifics shortly. Pynchon, in turn, belied his reputation and showed he did not see the impression that he had been making. Indeed, he revealed, when replying to Smith at the end of the month, that he had been waiting for advice, remarking that he agreed with Smith about the typescript's need of work and noting, "I am not (I hope) a 'temperamental author' and I am not about to buck at any suggestions" (August 31, 1961).

16   The less formal "Tom," interestingly, appears in the more formally grammatical rendition of the greeting, as a comma appears after "Hi" on Sleazus's shirt but not on the actual Penguin give-away.

17   The footage appeared on CNN, but Pynchon was not identified.

18   Pynchon himself, at least once, described himself as a recluse, noting in his June 2, 1963, letter to Faith Sale, "one of the advantages in being a recluse is that you can make your own plans, and barring war or natural catastrophe, comply with them." At the time, Pynchon was living alone, and the plans he was discussing involved visiting Kirkpatrick and Faith Sale in Ghana, where the two were headed. Pynchon gave up being a recluse when Tharaldsen arrived in Mexico and in his life at the end of 1963 or the beginning of 1964. If he had been serious about visiting Ghana, her arrival disrupted the freedom he had had to make his own plans (see Kachka 52 for the Pynchon–Tharaldsen relationship).

19   Henry Veggian notes, for example, "when Benny [Profane] first arrives in New York [. . .] scenes from Bernstein's 'West Side Story'" (226n298) are repeated.

20   Gordon dates his meeting the woman sometime in the fall of 1966 and his meeting Pynchon in June of 1967, a few years after

Pynchon began *Gravity's Rainbow*—if he began it shortly after *V.*'s publication, as is widely believed—and around the time he signed the contract for it with Viking. (For the date of the contract, January 24, 1967, see Howard.)

21   Discussing his "impatience with fiction [he] felt [. . .] to be 'too autobiographical,'" in his introduction to *Slow Learner*, Pynchon observes, "Somewhere I had come up with the notion that one's personal life had nothing to do with fiction, when the truth, as everyone knows, is nearly the direct opposite" (21).

22   I am playing off of Barthes's description of the photograph as "literally an emanation of the referent" (80), something that is not "a 'copy' of reality, but [. . .] an emanation of *past reality*: a *magic*, not an art" (88).

23   David Foster Wallace, in "Borges on the Couch," describes the biographer's inclination to find "personal stuff encoded in the writer's art" as "a syndrome that seems common to literary biographies, so common that it might point to a design flaw in the whole enterprise."

24   J. K. Trotter calls *Bleeding Edge* "something of a homecoming" in his review for the *Atlantic Wire*.

25   Entropy is itself a dual concept, simultaneously capable of being presented as chaos, that is, as a lack of cohesion, and as order, that is, a completely uniform stasis; the downstairs/upstairs division in Pynchon's short story, a division between exhausted searching and a sort of peace perhaps, presents the two ways of viewing the concept. (See note 92 for a further exploration of the dual quality of entropy.)

26   Pynchon, according to a 1965 "Between Issues" feature, told those in the offices of the *New Leader* to whom Sale introduced him that he was sleeping on a "pad in Kirk's bathtub" (2).

27   The identification, likely made while he was in the early stages of conceiving the character, that Pynchon constructs between himself and Stencil is complicated by the fact that there was a Stencil aboard the ship Pynchon served on, the *USS Hank*, when he was in the navy. That Stencil "was the Chief-of-the-Boat," that is, the master chief petty officer, as Tomaske (May 10, 2001), who made the discovery, told Corlies Smith. "And it turns out ah, he ah, he was what the other sailors called, 'Old Navy,' and they all lived in fear of him. He was a tattooed, um, hard-drinking sailor who could ah, in one sentence, reduce them to tears or just slap 'em around to the point where they were so afraid of him . . . that they would do anything he ordered."

While the biographical Stencil's reported character has little in common with the fictional character named Stencil, the Stencil in the navy seems to have been behind the incident that inspired *V*.'s *Scaffold's* broken propeller that left the ship stranded in Malta. When Pynchon's ship was leaving Norfolk at the beginning of the Suez Crisis, Stencil saw a hatch cover on the deck and ordered it removed. The crew tossed it over the side and hit and damaged a propeller, obliging the captain to dock in Malta to get a new propeller when the Mediterranean fleet was called to evacuate Americans from Egypt. The ship was placed on blocks, and a spotlight was put on the American flag so that Egyptian bombers wouldn't target it, exactly the way the *Scaffold* is described as docked in Malta (426). Is there a connection between the function of master chief petty officer, the senior enlisted man, on a ship; *V*.'s Stencil; and the novelist or storyteller? Pynchon was, we can imagine, amused by the idea that the man who served as the immediate source of order for the ship's other enlisted men was named Stencil, a word that means "a pattern, or a device used to create a pattern" (Hurley 151–52) and thus a name that is "entirely appropriate for someone who seeks to impose structure on the potential chaos of experience" (Grant 25). That an element of the story about Stencil's attempting to maintain a well-ordered deck but putting the ship out of commission made it into *V.* is perhaps telling.

28   For the relevance of the much-discussed Oedipa connection, see note 70 below. Mucho's connection is more tangential. Mathew Winston was told—truthfully or not—by someone that Pynchon "thought about becoming a disc jockey, an interest," Winston goes on to note, "which emerges in the character of Mucho" (51–52). Pynchon authorized the rumor, maybe from the beginning but certainly after the appearance of Winston's article. He begins a 1978 letter to a young novelist in the following manner: "What are you doing wrong? Don't ask me. I stumbled into this whole business 20 years ago when all I wanted to be was a disk jockey" (May 21, 1978). Mucho's time as a used car salesman also has an autobiographical association. George Stevens, a Lippincott executive, told Cork Smith, upon reading "Low-lands" after Smith had accepted it for publication in *New World Writing*, "I don't know what you like about this thing. I think this guy will be selling used Chevrolets within a year" (Silverman 157).

29   Speaking of Pynchon at the launch party for an exhibit of signed Pynchon first editions at UCLA, Gebauer recalled, "He's a great charades player. He's great at puns. They're awful" (see Kellogg).

30   Richard H. Blum observes in his monumental study *Society and Drugs*, "the straight and hippie worlds share a common belief that they stand opposed and distant from each other" (351). The distinction between the two worlds is, of course, not so straightforward and relies partly on a perspective derived from intuition rather than careful analysis. Pseudonymous former addict Andrew Reese, for instance, observes that for drug users, "the straight symbolizes the dominant society" (8), even though he also acknowledges at the time he is writing, the mid-1970s, that "the lines defining the user and the straight person are becoming blurred" (6) due to the fashionableness of drug use.

31   In the movie trailer, the clip in which Coy raises the question of whose side he is on is followed by a clip in which Doc says, "Good question," though the two clips are from different parts of the movie.

32   That Denis seems not to have addressed Smilin Steve by name in the drugstore is a marker of Denis's felt exclusion from the environment.

33   I'd like to thank Roy Benjamin for drawing my attention to this interview.

34   Pynchon also plays with a pun on "head" in *Vineland*, where the teenage head of A & R at Indolent Records screams, "Department *head!* [. . .] everybody around here's a department . . . *head!* Ha! Ha! Ha!" (283). Here, the many "heads" suggest a loss of cohesion to the enterprise, that is, the loss of community or the emergence of an entropic communal body—or corporate body in the sense in which Norman O. Brown uses the term in *Love's Body* (see 128)—that is composed of isolated heads without any members, making it impossible to envisage "an energy diffused throughout the whole body, and capable of displacement from one part to another" (Brown 127).

35   The verbal echo establishes an association between Pynchon's understanding of Winston and Julia's relationship and his fashioning of Coy and Hope's. The association is negative. In *Nineteen Eighty-Four* (1949), we have a trajectory, Pynchon writes, from "boy dislikes girl, boy and girl meet cute, first thing you know boy and girl are in love, then they get separated, finally they get back together. This is what transpires . . . sort of. But there's no happy ending" (xxii). In Orwell's novel, as Pynchon reads it, love, a revolutionary energy, provides an illusory escape from the all-encompassing tyranny of the novel's culture, but that tyranny is capable, expectedly, of crushing that love. In *Inherent Vice*, boy and girl meet squalid—despite

cuteness being everywhere and love being invoked, as in Orwell, to counter cultural hegemony—and their relationship's development is woven into the tyranny, that is, the addiction, that controls them. They, too, separate. Coy embraces the tyranny represented through Vigilant California by the Golden Fang, an organization that is analogous to Big Brother in that it seeks to have a controlling hand in all aspects of American life, including, as a supplier of heroin, the drug culture. Coy and Hope, however, get back together, reuniting for that happy ending that is missing in *Nineteen Eighty-Four*. Their reunion suggests a cute coming together that is capable of countering the forces of control, despite the overuse of the word "love," which not only renders it practically meaningless but also enables it to be coopted for the sake of control, for example, for "hustling people into sex activities they might not, given the choice, much care to engage in" (*IV* 5).

The echo that establishes the association between Coy and Hope and Winston and Julia can be traced back to *Gravity's Rainbow*, where Roger and Jessica have "what Hollywood likes to call a 'cute meet'" (38). The war takes on the guise of Big Brother, though a feminized version: "she *is* Roger's mother" (39). The trope emerges after Jessica's quip "Does your mother know *you're* out like this" (39), that is, does the controlling force in your life know what you're doing? Their love leads them to find a refuge, hidden from the mother's view: "It is marginal, hungry, chilly—most times they're too paranoid to risk a fire—but it's something they want to keep, so much that to keep it they will take on more than propaganda has ever asked them for. They are in love. Fuck the war" (41–42), "an attitude [that] cannot," Herman and Weisenburger observe, "overcome [the couple's] dependence on the conflict. They wouldn't be together without the war" (108), much as there would be no Coy–Hope without heroin addiction or Winston–Julia without Big Brother. The war, of course, proves more like Big Brother than like heroin addiction, for the love that depends on it doesn't develop into a happy ending: the war's dissolution leads to their love's passing, as if even the drugs that have a negative connotation in Pynchon's oeuvre retain something positive about them, at least when compared to war or totalitarian regimes.

36   Indeed, according to Chrissie Wexler, Pynchon "broke up more than one marriage, because he was too shy to find someone on his own. He made friends with couples and went off with the wife" (*Lineland* 78). Tharaldsen confirmed this observation, telling Kachka, "That seems to be his *modus operandi*. [...] It's a pattern" (153).

37   Pynchon told Sale he had just found out that Thelonius Monk's middle name was Sphere. He was concerned that he would have to change the name of the character Sphere in *V.* for legal reasons.

38   Pynchon's question to Siegel, "Why should things be easy to understand?" (*Lineland* 115), might thus be reformulated as "Why must things be hard to understand?" with the implied answer being that working through the difficulty facilitates one's ability to get past the shallow liberty afforded by easy pleasures and achieve genuine freedom.

39   For a discussion of the domestication of hippies on television, see Aniko Bodroghkozy's *Groove Tube* (61–92). Bodroghkozy's interest is in how television sought to sanitize hippies' image and thereby accustom viewers to their presence. Pynchon's Bigfoot commercials draw on that sanitizing function, but they also present suburban housing estates to hippies so that the lifestyle associated with suburban homes can be accommodated to the counterculture and hippies can be duped into domesticating themselves.

40   To counteract the tolerance one immediately builds up to LSD, one could double the dosage the following day, but the amount of acid one would need to take to trip daily would quickly become a problem. The tolerance does wear off after a few days. For the fantasy, see Tom Burke, "Princess Leda's Castle in the Air," an article—originally appearing in the March 1970 issue of *Esquire*—that investigates L.A.'s cult scene in 1970 in the aftermath of the murder of Sharon Tate and briefly touches on the paranoia of the police with regard to cults: a Beverly Hills policeman, "several weeks before" Charles Manson was arrested, asserts, "When they find the killer, they'll find him to be a doper and a hellhound," that is, one of the "Satanist dope fiends" (308) he claims are destroying the town. Another of Burke's sources, "a singer of some note[—who] asks not to be identified" (305) and who is marginally involved, her comments suggest, in the cult scene, the emergence of which she attributes to regular acid consumption—observes, "Ken Kesey finally saw what would happen as a result of daily tripping. Even Leary has begun to dig it...." (306). The central figure of the piece, Leda, also claims to "drop acid daily" and believes she is about to replace Timothy Leary, a "misuser of sacred chemicals," as the "spiritual leader" of the counterculture: "I give acid to persons who have never dropped it without telling them. I think of this as the administering of Holy

Communion" (311). She is a dark version of Vehi, who gives Doc acid without clearly telling him what he is getting.

41   The connection between the period about which Pynchon is writing and the period in which Garfield's 1951 movie appeared is historically apt: both periods are at the end of their particular eras. As Louis Menand observes about the late 1940s and early 1950s in a discussion of Jack Kerouac's *On The Road* (1957), "The bits and pieces of America that the book captures [between 1947 and 1950, when Kerouac took the road trips the book is based on] are carefully selected to represent a way of life that is coming to an end in the postwar boom, a way of life before televisions and washing machines and fast food, when millions of people lived patched-together existences and men wandered the country—'ramblin' round,' in the Guthrie song—following the seasons in search of work. [. . .] [T]hey are pictures of a world not yet made plump and uniform by postwar affluence and consumerism."

42   Note the contrast here with Pynchon's comments on an advantage to reclusiveness in his June 2, 1963, letter to Faith Sale (see note 18 above).

43   For a discussion of the 1960s as a liminal period, see Freer (25–37).

44   Bill Roeder, reporting on the existence of both projects in 1978, notes that Pynchon was said to have "walked the 233-mile length of the Mason-Dixon line" (7) for research purposes.

45   Pynchon told Kirkpatrick and Faith Sale (March 27, 1964) at the time that he was working on four projects but getting nowhere with any of them and revealed that his going to Berkeley following Farina's wedding was spurred by his interest in returning to college to study math. The shock of the Kennedy assassination coupled with personal stress (perhaps having to do with his attraction to Tharaldsen) almost led him to give up on writing, but his being turned down by Berkeley led him to think there wasn't anything else for him to do.

46   Pynchon wrote two undated letters to Stephens, who had contacted him about Tomasz Mirkowicz. Mirkowicz wanted Pynchon's permission to translate his work into Polish, probably in the early to mid-eighties and likely around the time Melanie Jackson was shopping *Slow Learner* to publishers, given the frustration Pynchon expresses over his dealings with the publishing industry.

47   Concern over giving up one's ideals to pursue wealth can be found in the construction of Peter Pinguid's biography in *The Crying*

of Lot 49. After participating, however mock-heroically, in "the very first military confrontation between Russia and America [. . . Pinguid becomes] our first casualty" (50). He does not die; rather, he "[v]iolated his upbringing and code of honor [. . .] and for the rest of his life he did little more than acquire wealth" (51), in short, abandoning the struggle. Discussing *Mason & Dixon* in relation to "Is It O.K. to Be a Luddite?" David Cowart locates the issue in Pynchon's concern with "the struggle between scientific rationalism and the perennial yearning for mystical possibility" (139). To replace that yearning with the pursuit of capitalistic gain, capitalism having inevitably led to Marxism, as Mike Fallopian asserts (*CL49* 51), is to give up on the potential offered by "Worlds alternative to this one" (*M&D* 359).

48   Pynchon has thwarted easy closure since *V.*, ending that novel with Stencil's heading off to investigate another lead—even though certain readers might have begun to think that he has followed his mystery to her dissolution—and with Profane's being stuck on Malta without a clear plan about how to get back home. The fantasy that closes the completion of the line in *Mason & Dixon* is a continuation of the trend, Pynchon's interests being like young folks: "What is most appealing about [them], after all, is the changes, not the still photograph of finished character but the movie, the soul in flux" (*SL* 23). Pynchon's decision to keep his image and life story out of the media may be, in part, an attempt to avoid being reduced to a still photograph or the narrative equivalent of one.

49   Although written while Pynchon was away from New York, the letter to Barthelme suggests Pynchon had been in New York the previous two or so years, and it was during this period that he first became involved with Melanie Jackson.

50   Kirkpatrick Sale is likely the source for the sentence in the Dudar article. Kachka notes that "Pynchon broke off contact after Sale talked to a reporter" (157; see also Portinari), and Dudar's article is the first one since a few that appeared in the wake of *V.* for which a writer managed to get information about Pynchon from his friends. Dudar reports, "If [Pynchon] is camping in your house for a spell, he may quarrel with your preschool child about the television shows they will watch; his tastes run to the sort of junk embraced by any addict committed to pop culture" (35); Sale told Kachka that he remembers Pynchon "arguing with his kids over which cartoons to watch" (153). Sale—who was in the same circle as Barthelme—and Pynchon may not have been in regular contact in the period

in which Sale spoke with Dudar, even though Pynchon seems to have been in New York in the early eighties. Different interests may have just not given them much reason to get together. Sale may even have talked for that reason. If Sale was a source for some of the information about Pynchon more contemporary to Dudar's article, Sale may have been passing on some secondhand information, the rumors circulating about Pynchon in the early eighties among those with whom he associated around the time *Gravity's Rainbow* was published.

51   After Pynchon completed the manuscript of *Gravity's Rainbow*, his place of residence wasn't as stable as it had been when he lived in Manhattan Beach, but the evidence suggests he did not live out of hotels, as Kachka suggests (see 158). Pynchon was in New York in the year before the publication of *Gravity's Rainbow*, when he stayed at the Sales' place in Manhattan; he left for the West coast in the Fall of 1973 but was back in New York in January of 1974 and was up around Middletown, NY, later that year (see Blumenthal), a region he seems to have stayed in for a while. He became friends with Richard Connolly, an English professor at Rockland Community College (RCC), who introduced him to Jay Carter England, a jazz musician who also taught at RCC, and England's wife, Barbara. She was friends with a woman named Geraldine or became friends with her. Geraldine could be the girlfriend that Pynchon named in the Shetzline–Beal letter, and she may very well be the reason he was in the area.

In an email exchange between Norman England, Jay and Barbara's son, and Jonathan Glassow, an independent researcher, Norman England recalled Pynchon's dining at the England's house, spending a day with him and his brother at the Museum of Natural History in NYC, and attending a local concert. Norman has two interesting memories of Pynchon. At the end of their time at the museum,

> Tom said "Norman, people love stories. They thrive on them. But you have to give them something to use that will spark their interest and give them something to work with. For example, if we were to walk through the museum with limps, it's a kind of storytelling. People will look at us and try to figure out in their mind the story behind our limps. Say, why don't we do that? Why don't we walk through the museum with funny limps?" So, each of us [including Norman's brother] came up with some strange kind of walk. I was pulling my right leg

along as if the foot was dead weight. My mom said she couldn't figure out what the 3 of us were doing when she came to pick us up because we were all walking in a weird, ridiculous way.

The other memory involved the local concert, which was the last time Norman saw Pynchon:

> I had on a *Star Trek* windbreaker that you could order from the side of the Enterprise plastic model kit. My dad used to give me a hard time for wearing it, but when Tom saw it he said, "Wow! Is that a *Star Trek* jacket? Where did you get that? I want one!" It was the first time I'd heard an adult get excited about *Star Trek*. My dad would tell me how Tom was the greatest writer in America, yet here he was into what I was into. (Private correspondence)

Pynchon seems to have stuck around the East coast until sometime in 1975. Smith told Tomaske that Pynchon occasionally went to dinner with him and his wife, Sheila, and Donadio as well, in the '70s. Pynchon may have moved to Berkely, CA, by the spring of 1975—that is, early enough to appear in that year's phone book—at least he did if the Tyrone Slothrop that Thomas Schaub played bridge with was Pynchon. He showed up in Trinidad, CA, around 1976 and stayed there until 1977 (Kachka 154; Glassow, who is Kachka's "Pynchon tracker"). He was in England around the time Larry Kramer's *Faggots* (1978) was published, both Christopher Hitchens and Tom Maschler (96–97) reveal, returning to the U.S. sometime in 1979 (see Hitchens 1985 772). He likely remained in New York for a good part of the next few years. It was apparently in this period, in 1980 or 1981, that he began dating Melanie Jackson. Donadio "told others Pynchon had been staying in Donadio's apartment (platonically)" when that relationship, almost certainly without her knowing about it, began (Kachka 154). He may have moved in with Jackson after that arrangement fell apart.

52   The letter in which Pynchon informs Donadio that she is no longer his agent is dated January 5, 1982 (see Gussow). The break came after Donadio fired Jackson for reasons Corlies Smith, perhaps disingenuously, told Tomaske (August 3, 2001) were "apparently alien" to her relationship with Pynchon. Still, the inference one is led to make is that Pynchon left Donadio over her firing of Jackson, although he avoided putting it that way to Smith at a lunch Smith had arranged

to discuss what had happened. Smith told Tomaske the lunch was perfectly friendly, but he made Herman think—in a separate interview, conducted in preparation for the work Herman and Krafft have done on the *V.* typescript—that he "understood that P[ynchon] also wanted to get rid of him because he was part of the past with Candida" ("Notes on the Interview"). Indeed, Smith told Tomaske that the lunch was "phony" because the topic of Jackson was not raised, and partially contradicting what he said about the Jackson–Pynchon connection being alien to Donadio's reason for firing Jackson, Smith revealed to Herman, according to Herman's paraphrase of his June 7, 2001, interview with Smith, "first, that Candida's accountant had told her that Melanie was bringing in restaurant bills on a daily basis that had obviously nothing to do with work (and which in retrospect may have enhanced her anger)." These receipts, which Tracy Daugherty describes as "Chinese take-out receipts" (366), may have had something to do with her lunching with Pynchon, as Karen Hudes suggests (158) "[S]econd," Herman also notes that "Melanie, when invited to Candida's house in Stonington, had asked her whether she could bring 'a date,' that Candida had accepted and that this date turned out to be none other than Pynchon" (Notes on Interview). Harriet Wasserman gave Tomaske, as well as Herman, a different account of the incident, telling Tomaske (June 28, 2001) that Pynchon had asked Donadio if he could bring a date. "And the next thing she knew, she got a phone call from the Mystic train station saying, 'Hi Candida. It's me. Guess who the friend is.'" Pynchon didn't tell Smith any version of these stories. Rather, he complained that Donadio hadn't "done anything for [him] in the last few years." Smith asked, "What was there to do?" Pynchon answered that "[s]he hasn't done anything with movies." Smith then observed, "'From my understanding, you didn't want a movie made.' He wanted," Smith went on to explain, "script approval [apparently for a *Crying of Lot 49* movie]—God doesn't get script approval in Hollywood" (quoted in Hudes 158–59).

Whatever happened—and both Smith and Wasserman may have been repeating rumors when telling about the incident at Donadio's house in Stonington—Pynchon became Jackson's first client. The first book she would shop around, in 1982 or early 1983, was the collection of short stories that was published as *Slow Learner* in 1984. During this time, Pynchon broke off his professional relationship with Smith and Viking, with whom he had signed a million-dollar, two-book contract in 1976, receiving $50,000 a year for the first three years after signing it. Jackson called Smith about the collection, giving Viking a chance to bid on it, but when Smith made an offer of $25,000, Melanie told him that another publisher had said $135,000. Viking proved willing to match that figure, but Jackson was unwilling to take it, telling Smith she had an offer for $150,000, the figure Dudar reported (36), perhaps on Smith's authority, that Pynchon had been paid. During the Herman interview, Smith seems to have begun to speculate, without explicitly expressing the idea, that Pynchon might have wanted to buy out his contract with Viking. The possibility that such was the case leads one to wonder what Pynchon discussed with Viking president Irving Goodman in spring 1983 (see Dudar 36). Could Pynchon have used the $150,000 or a part of it to free himself from his contractual obligation to Viking, allowing him to publish his next books with whomever he wanted?

53 Both Dudar and Kachka mention that Pynchon watched a lot of television. See also "That Which Has Seemingly Influenced Thomas Pynchon," an article that tells the following anecdote: "It seems that Pynchon's sister Judith once taught at Suffolk Community College and a colleague of [John Krafft, who taught at Suffolk in the 1980s,] actually dated her, and asked her, one time, 'What's your brother likely to be doing right now?' and she said, "Watching *The Brady Bunch.*' [. . .] [I]t's Pynchon's favorite show. So, Tom is just like you and me! He watches cruddy TV!" The source for this story is Krafft, though the Pomona retelling of it is botched, for Krafft's recounting of it to me is as follows: "I had a colleague (he had arrived at Suffolk in 1974 and did not date Judith) who told me he once asked Judith ... etc. But I remember her answer as 'Probably watching *The Brady Bunch*. It's his favorite show'" (private correspondence). The incident probably happened not long after 1974. Coincidentally, Krafft had met, a couple of years before going to teach at Suffolk Community College, someone else, a colleague at a different college, who had dated Pynchon's sister while he had taught at Suffolk. The Pomona article combines the two colleagues.

54 Hector may have allowed his tubal addiction to destroy his marriage—"the television set, a 19-inch French Provincial floor model, [having been named] as correspondent" (348) in his divorce proceedings—but he continues to long for his wife. Dancing with Frenesi in Vegas, "Hector was interested to find himself with a hardon, not for Frenesi who was here, but for Debbi who wasn't, that girl in the Mormon makeup who'd always held the pink slip to his

heart, and the memory of the last time they'd danced together, to the radio, in the kitchen, with the lights off, and the night of love and sex strangely as always intermingled" (350).

55   The drug destroys Hope and Coy's marriage as well as limits, Doc speculates, Shasta's options during her time with him at Gordita beach: "Doc, aside from being just about the only doper she knew who didn't use heroin, which freed up a lot of time for both of them, had never figured out what else she might've seen in him" (11).

56   See Brian McHale for an analysis of the ambiguity of the novel's treatment of television (116–25).

57   For a discussion of the use of and battle over obscenity laws, see Herman and Weisenburger (51–58).

58   The explanation is a simplification to be sure but one that is presented with more nuance in *Vineland*, where the People's Republic of Rock and Roll serves as a microcosm of the period's counterculture and reminds us that it wasn't necessarily a cohesive thing.

59   The Golden Fang's interest in dentistry is also to the point, though Doc does not explicitly bring it to the reader's attention. Anderson's film does so, however. In the movie, Hope's discussion of the effects of heroin on the teeth is read by the voice-over narrator while Doc explores Blatnoyd's offices.

60   The control Golden Fang/Vigilant California seeks to wield is, in a sense, analogous to heroin addiction. Bigfoot's commercials, however, imply that even local alternatives can be coopted. (For a discussion of Bigfoot's commercials, see 37–38 above.)

61   In *Bleeding Edge*, Reg observes that a similar problem is posed by the Internet, a medium Pynchon presents as a source now of freedom and now of control at different times in his work: "Future of film if you want to know—someday, more bandwidth, more video files up on the Internet, everybody'll be shootin everything, way too much to look at, nothin will mean shit" (143).

Note that Pynchon writes "rock and roll" in Mucho's dialogue rather than "rock 'n' roll." The formality is perhaps an indication that the music has been coopted. If so, *Vineland* registers disillusionment with a genre of music that had been regarded as oppositional from its beginnings in the fifties. The informal "rock 'n' roll" is used exclusively in *Slow Learner* and *Bleeding Edge*, while *Vineland* has "rock and roll" throughout. Both spellings are used in *Inherent Vice*, the formal "and" appearing just twice, the first time in a sentence uttered by Bigfoot

(139) and the second in a sentence from the *Golden Fang Procedures Handbook* (170) in Dr. Blatnoyd's office.

62   J. Kerry Grant has observed that Oedipa may not have attended Cornell, noting that her description of her college as "a somnolent Siwash" (103) "suggests otherwise" (10), for a siwash is, "[a]ccording to the *New Dictionary of American Slang,* 'Any small college; the archetypical small college'" (Grant 80). "Siwash," however, seems to be used metaphorically and is, therefore, capitalized; in comparison to campuses like that of Berkeley in the 1960s, the 1950s' campus of even a large university like Cornell seems like that of a siwash.

63   John Krafft reports being told that bringing a date out at sunrise was a seduction ruse at Cornell in the fifties (private correspondence), a notion that fits in with the idea that the sunrise Oedipa recalls no one seeing can be read as an unrecognized harbinger of what was to come, which includes the sexual revolution.

64   Oedipa recalls earlier encounters with the disenfranchised but sees new significance in them while she wanders the track.

65   The Golden Fang's connection to Coy's situation also implies an association between it and the countersubversive community, Vigilant California in particular, just as its connection to Wolfmann's disappearance implies an association between it and the Feds, one that may be undermined by the seizure of the schooner *Golden Fang* at the novel's close.

66   The criminal connotations of this underworld and Doc's ability to facilitate escape from it are implied because it is during the zombie episode that we learn Jade's real name, Ashley, and find out something substantial about her. She thereby develops into something more than a simple low-level stock figure of the Los Angeles underworld. She has a backstory and a real name, just like a real person.

67   The Feds' presence is also tied into Charlock's murder. Special Agents Flatweed and Borderline are "investigating Black Nationalist Hate Groups" (74), and Charlock was setting up the small-arms deal with Tariq and his "people, Warriors Against the Man Black Armed Militia (WAMBAM)" (292).

68   In his forward to Orwell's *Nineteen Eighty-Four*, Pynchon confirms *Vineland's* take on "crime dramas," which he notes are "themselves forms of social control" (xv), but his characterization of Bigfoot complicates that position. Bigfoot's humanity is allowed to come through, but he acts as if his job requires him to conceal it. There is a comparable moment in *Vineland,* when Hector complains

that Zoyd hasn't asked him about his wife and children, but the point is different. Hector, who is unsuccessful at manipulating the ritual to turn Zoyd, tries another approach, attempting to develop intimacy, but that approach, particularly at the moment we observe it, is a ruse. Hector is divorced, cut off from his family in his tubal fantasy, but he must have sought to develop such intimacy to turn Zoyd, who already knows, it is clear, about Debbi and the children.

69   Anderson's film may put Adrian Prussia at the scene: the hand holding the bat that knocks Doc out seems to be Prussia's.

70   Oedipa is a "Young Republican" (76), and despite the apparent leftist leanings of the articles Pynchon published in high school (see below 79–86), he may have been one as well, at least informally. He grew up in a Republican household: his father was a prominent Republican in Oyster Bay, serving as the town's Republican leader for a time and, from 1959 to 1962, as the Superintendent of Highways, the position he held when he was appointed Town Supervisor at the end of 1962 (see *New York Times* December 5, 1962). Pynchon Sr. failed to win the election the following year due to a scandal over an asphalt company's overcharging the town during his tenure as superintendent and his receiving gifts—including box seats for the World Series, meals, turkeys, and flowers—from the company, some of which he obliquely admitted to taking: "I received some poinsettias and I managed to keep one alive, and it will give me great pleasure to put one on your political grave" ("L.I. Aide Concedes Possible Padding" 45), he told Milton Lipson, the Democratic county commissioner of accounts, who was investigating the allegations against him.

If Pynchon identified as a Republican in his youth, he seems to have retained some of his conservative leanings into the early 1960s, which a December 1, 1962, letter to Bob Hillock, a friend whom he worked with at Boeing, seems to suggest. Pynchon observes,

> I suppose you are deliriously happy about [George] Romney winning [the governorship] in Michigan. If that bastard is elected president (or even nominated) I'm leaving the country and *staying* away. The GOP screwed up once, in '52, as you know, by nominating that drooling imbecile what's-his-name instead of a legitimate conservative like Taft. They are reaping the results, namely an irresponsible and possibly lunatic right wing. Nominating Romney is only going to compound the

felony: Romney is nothing but a organization man, a technician without principles. [...] If the GOP nominates Romney, it will mean they've decided to adopt a Democratic identity. And that means renouncing the only identity they can honestly have nowadays: that of a responsibly conservative party.

While Pynchon could be presenting an older conservatism in a positive light here to appeal to his friend's politics, even though he denounces the Republican Party under Dwight D. Eisenhower as well as the extreme right, Pynchon seems more concerned with the dismantling of the diffrence between the two parties, a problem that gives the extreme right the opportunity to emerge as a stronger force of political opposition. Indeed, despite what Pynchon says about the Democratic Party, he isn't opposed to it: he reminds Hillock in a letter dated April 11, 1964, that he had a favorable view of John F. Kennedy. Romney's possible rise to the presidency is dangerous because Romney will, Pynchon fears, lead the Republican Party to more closely mirror the Democratic Party, when Republicans should serve as a responsible opposition to it. Both sides are necessary: hence Pynchon observes that he would feel just as traumatized by an Eisenhower assassination as he is by Kennedy's. "The logic being that political murders should not be part of a civilized democracy."

Pynchon remained interested in the direction in which the Republican Party was headed, mentioning to Donadio in September of 1963 the idea of covering the 1964 Republican Convention. His interest in the idea may have been half-hearted. He told Hillock he hadn't thought "anything would come of it," but after Kennedy's assassination, he grew more pessimistic, wondering "what can I possibly say about the Republican covention that would be of any use to anybody." He, nonetheless, continued to solicit information about the direction the party is taking, telling Hillock, "Hey, about these caucuses, I wish you'd write and tell me what's been going on, in as much detail as you'd care to; [...] I'm still interested in the subject and would like to hear about any tilts you may be having with the far right" (April 11, 1964). The turn toward the far right that the nomination of Barry Goldwater for the presidency at the Republican Convention illustrated likely turned Pynchon against the party, or further against it if his favorable view of Kennedy suggests he was already becoming disillusioned with conservatism. He, after all, would have liked and expected "to see old Barry get put down" (April 11, 1964).

71   Pynchon acquired a P.O. Box address in Aptos in 1983, likely after the road trip he mentioned to Barthelme. He seems to have been establishing residency in Northern California at the time, getting a driver's license on May 10, 1983, and living there presumably during the mid-eighties, although he returned to New York regularly, "spending six months on the West Coast and six months in New York" (8-D), Kevin Galvin reported, likely to see Jackson, whom he married at the end of the decade. In fact, he returned to the East coast for a short period almost immediately after leaving. Discussing his spring 1983 lunch with Pynchon, Goodman told Dudar that Pynchon "had been traveling—I don't know where—and was in New York for about two weeks" (see note 52 above). Pynchon, in any case, shows a familiarity with Northern California, adapting the names of establishments in Humboldt County in *Vineland*. For example, the Jambalaya Restaurant, an eatery and music venue in Arcata, CA, becomes the novel's Humbalaya, Jonathan Glassow observes (private correspondence).

72   What led Pynchon to submit a statement of purpose, not an application per say, to the Ford Foundation Program for the Humanities and Arts grant—which would pay $7,500 each to writers, poets or fiction writers who would be attached to an opera or theater company for a year with the hope, not obligation, that they would write a libretto or play—is more surprising than Weisenburger reveals. Tomaske, who discovered the Pynchon document and unsuccessfully sought permission to publish it through Pynchon's agent, also got access to the entire Foundation file for the 1959 program. The process the Foundation followed to find writers, these documents show, was to seek nominations, asking "240 writers, critics, musicians, publishers and others professionally engaged in the theatrical or literary world [...] to nominate not more than two poets or novelists for the program" (quoted in Tomaske's Notes for a Paper). Pynchon did not apply on his own initiative for a grant that stipulated that the writers who would be awarded it be proven talents. Someone, likely one of his professors, the name of whom the Foundation file does not record, nominated Pynchon, and the autobiographical statement Weisenburger discusses was written in response to material Pynchon received from the Foundation.

73   "Classical" is used loosely here to mean orthodox or academic, a looseness Pynchon employed well into the eighties, writing in his review of Gabriel Garcia Marquez's *Love in The Time of Cholera* (1985,

1988) that "the Garcimarquesian voice we have come to recognize from the other fiction has matured, found and developed new resources, been brought to a level where it can at once be classical and familiar."

74   Jules Feiffer, in *Sick, Sick, Sick,* a comic strip that began appearing in the *Village Voice* in 1956 and a collection of strips published as a book in 1958, satirizes the conformist quality to those identifying themselves as nonconformists. Two strips from the book portray the nonconforming posture as something that can be manipulated as a marketing tool: a writer ponders writing a book about "his withdrawal" and selling it so that "everyone makes a mint," and an adman outlines a campaign to take the angry-young-man rage and "merchandise it in useful ways." Another strip satirizes the emphasis on knowing the latest anti-establishment lingo, referring to the latest hip term as the right "password," which one must be aware of to avoid being ostracized. One strip refers specifically to the Beats: a man laments his inability to be "beat," that is, to grow sideburns, like "jazz and motor scooters," and alter his "speech patterns." "What I wouldn't give to be a non-conformist like all those others," he laments (n.pp.).

75   Sale's draft has Hero describe himself as "a singer, just a singer" (Act 1, scene 1), so the apparent allusion to Fariña is absent.

76   Uncle Chauncey is not in Pynchon's list of characters. Sale, presumably later, attempted to draft an Uncle Chauncey song, though only the first and last of the four verses have more than a line or two.

77   Pynchon, besides giving Broad the regional-coordinator title, has her make it known that she has dealt with groups similar to the minstrels before (Act 1, scene 2). In Sale's draft, the island's minstrels are the first of their kind that she has encountered: "I have heard in our history tapes about people such as you," she notes, "but I never believed any really existed" (Act 1, scene 1).

78   The material we have consists of Pynchon's handwritten draft of Act 1, scenes 1 and 2, and handwritten prefatory material that sets the scene for the action of the play; Sale's typed extensive outlines of Act 1, scene 3, Act 2, scenes 2 and 3, and Act 3, scene 1; Sale's typed draft of the scenes that Pynchon also drafted, with typed prefatory material; Pynchon's handwritten skeletal outlines of the entire musical, that is, the three acts with three scenes each; and drafts of songs, most of them handwritten, though not exclusively in Pynchon's hand.

Elements of this material strongly suggest that Sale's outlines and drafts were typed before Pynchon drafted his first two scenes, but after Sale and Pynchon discussed the content of the play and perhaps after Pynchon jotted down his own outlines, which contain only a few fragmented lines for each scene. That Sale did his work before Pynchon drafted his version of Act 1, scenes 1 and 2, as well as the probability that Pynchon had Sale's material in hand when writing those scenes, is revealed by Pynchon's including such references to the typed draft as the parenthetical note "Kirk's suggested pose," which is "She throws her head back, sticks her breasts out, spreads her feet" (S Act 1, scene 1), and by the presence of nearly identical lines in both versions.

Still, both similarities between Sale's drafts and outlines on the one hand and Pynchon's work on the other, and differences between Sale's outlines and his drafted scenes suggest that Sale must have brought to his work some notion of the content to which he was setting out to give form. Even the use of placeholder names is revealing. Pynchon usually skips naming the main characters in his outlines; Broad and Hero are mostly referred to as "girl" and "boy," though the names Hero, Prostitute, Sailmaker, Jazzman, Dud Bomber, Tube Tester, and Johnny Badass, who is also called IBM Hero in the notes to Act 1, scene 3, are scattered throughout. Pynchon even mentions a jazz group, the plan for which indicates that Sale's having more than one Jazzman makes more sense than Pynchon's having only one. Sale, in his outlines, uses placeholders that are either the same as or similar to the ones appearing in Pynchon's, but Sale attempts to establish realistic names in his drafts, calling Broad—a placeholder appearing first in his outline—Ivy and Johnny Badass Mr. x, a placeholder as well but one that acknowledges that the "Vice President in charge of the N.Y. area for IBM" (P Act 1, scene 2) should have a formal sounding name. Pynchon seems to have been unhappy with those choices, for he uses Broad and Johnny Badass in his drafts.

The most suggestive element of the differences is that the teddy bear that Hero gives to Broad in Pynchon's Act 1, scene 2, is a panda bear in Pynchon's outline as well as in Sale's outline of Act 3, scene 1. The only reference to a bear in Sale's version of Act 1, scene 2, is Pynchon's handwritten text above stage directions that follow a song sung by Hero, which Sale does not include, even though the carnival booth is, according to the prefatory material that sets the scene, "perhaps a knock-the-cat-off-win-a-teddy-bear booth," which is what appears in Pynchon's version of the scene. Pynchon's text on Sale's version reads, "goes behind booth, picks up teddy bear, gently gives it to the girl, then," stage directions that are meant to be inserted between the typed text "Hero" and "bends and kisses girl" and that correspond, except for the type of bear, to Pynchon's outline. Pynchon's full description of scene 2 is

> 2) Same setting
> Boy + girl meet – fall in love
> Girl of computer – feeds cards
> boy sings love song after they talk – he gives her panda.
> She's confused – he goes off – she ponders w/ machine.

Sale could have forgotten the bear when writing his draft. Its appearance in the outline of Sale's Act 3, scene 1, demonstrates that he knew Hero was to give one to Broad, and while Hero could give the panda bear to Broad in Sale's Act 2, scene 1, the description of which is lost, that is improbable. In Pynchon's outline of Act 2, scene 1, Broad is alone in her room, and it is likely that Pynchon and Sale had worked out the content of each scene before making the outlines, given that all the scenes we have from the two versions agree on the settings. The problem with accepting the assumption that Sale did not put off having Hero give the bear to Broad is that the stage direction in Pynchon's version of Act 1, scene 2, which appears just after Broad mentions the bear—that is, when she first arrives on the scene and asks Hero what he wants—reads, "real Jimmy Stewart. Lot of stuttering. Scratches head. Head, not armpit. Jimmy Stewart, ie, not Jimmy Dean." Explaining the distinction between the two Jimmies could imply that Sale had referenced the wrong actor in the lost text of his Act 2, scene 1, having decided to put off Hero's giving Broad a bear, and Pynchon is correcting him. Of course, if Sale wasn't as knowledgeable about movie stars as Pynchon, he could have confused the two actors in a conversation about the scene, leading Pynchon to emphasize the difference, or Pynchon could simply be indicating that he has changed his mind about what actor to reference. Hero, after all, "scratches armpit" after Broad tells him that his laziness, not the IBMers' rendering his profession unnecessary, is the cause of his unemployment.

Pynchon's change of the panda bear to a teddy bear, a change that Sale's description of the booth may have led him to consider, is more revealing: it demonstrates something about how his approach to the material differs from Sale's. Pynchon was likely aware that the teddy bear was named after Theodore Roosevelt. A Pynchon–Roosevelt connection was important enough to his father to warrant discussion in Pynchon Sr.'s obituary. "Ethel Roosevelt, T.R.'s daughter, was [Pynchon Sr.'s] Sunday school teacher. The Roosevelts and Pynchons were very close," John Gable, executive director of the Theodore Roosevelt Association, told Justin Martin for New York *Newsday*. "He [Pynchon Sr.] told me he remembered going to church on Sundays and saluting Mr. Roosevelt at his pew, and Mr. Roosevelt always saluted him back" (A10). Roosevelt was responsible for expanding the number of National Parks and came to be known as the "conservation president" (Wales and Lathrop 31) for the work he did to preserve unspoiled lands from the impact of modern life. Similarly, the minstrels want the IBMers to treat the island as a place apart in which elements of the past that modern living will destroy are preserved. Thus Hero tells Broad,

> All we want is someplace where every time we turn around we don't see that idiot damn machine staring at us. We're not hurting you people. We don't start revolutions, we don't preach any inflammatory doctrines. All we ask is to be left alone. Maybe by your standards we're wrong but for crying out loud, we're harmless. (Act 1, scene 2)

The teddy bear is an apt symbol of Hero's hope. The change from panda to teddy bear demonstrates how Pynchon looks to integrate the parts more meaningfully into the whole. Other differences between the two versions of the drafted scenes support such an assessment. For instance, Sale made the carnival booth the setting for the second scene but apparently did so indifferently or for a practical reason—to avoid having to bring new props on stage, since the booth is present in scene 1. Despite choosing the setting, Sale doesn't do anything with it in his version of the scene, which could be changed without significant changes to the action or dialogue. Pynchon, by contrast, integrates the scenery into the action and dialogue, chiefly by building a story around the teddy bear, and significant changes would need to be made if the scene were moved, say, to the front of a Ferris wheel. Similarly, the computer that the IBMers are planning to build on the island becomes in Pynchon's version "the Musical Unidirectional Force Field Equipped Tabulator. . . . Abbreviated MUFFET," which, of course, alludes to the nursery rhyme in which the proper Miss Muffet is thrown into confusion by the presence of a spider, a creature who does not acknowledge the world of propriety. The name of the computer evokes the action of the entire play, the disturbing of the social proprieties of the IBM world by the minstrels, symbolically the spider, albeit one whose powers are less obvious than that of the nursery-rhyme character. MUFFET, after all, is unlikely to be gotten off the island any time soon. The minstrels leave instead. Indeed, if this MUFFET is a precursor to the MUFFET in "Entropy," the "Multi-unit factorial field electronic tabulator" (90), that has Miriam, the apparently soon-to-be-ex-wife of Saul, "bugged at the idea of computers acting like people," such machines serve to drive away the bugs—the minstrels or Miriam—bugs whose presence raises questions about the machines' problematic power.

That is not to say that Sale was indifferent to the symbolic significance of the play's elements. His name for Broad (the chief secretary), Ivy, is itself symbolic. Johnny Badass is described as "pompous, very ivy dressed" in the description of Act 1, scene 3, suggesting that, for Sale, Ivy is short for Ivy League, making such universities (including Pynchon and Sale's own), symbolically speaking, secretaries to the powers that be in the culture at large. Sale, however, seems more interested in social commentary than in anything else, that is, in the message the play has for the audience, not in how the parts work with each other aesthetically. Pynchon is concerned with how the elements contribute to the play's symbolic network as well as its meaning, to create which he plays with allusions. The references to pop-cultural icons—Jimmy Stewart in Act 1, scene 2, Frank Sinatra in Act 3, scene 1—are meant to provide visual clues to help the audience better understand the scenes. The audience should recognize that Hero's movements mimic pop-cultural icons, drawing significance from the common late-fifties reading of their characteristic poses. Sale, by contrast, draws on cultural types, for example, the "mad ave fraternity boy" (Act 1, scene 3) and "the modern business woman" (Act 1, scene 1), to develop a realistic world meant to be immediately recognized so the audience can see the faults of its own world reflected in the musical's 1998 dystopia. The panda, just like the scenery in Act 1, scene 2, serves as nothing more than a prop in such an approach, so Sale neglects to include the bear when drafting the scene in which Hero is supposed to give it to Broad and leaves it as a panda in Act 3, despite his having written that the carnival booth could be a knock-the-cat-off-win-a-teddy-bear booth. (I'm assuming each of the outlines contains material introduced by the other collaborator, so Sale includes the Sinatra reference, which Pynchon's known predilection for drawing on pop culture suggests he would have used, in his outline for Act 3, scene 1, while Pynchon jots down the phrase "mad ave boy" in his outline to Act 1, scene 3.)

79   Broad/Ivy repeats the line in Sale's draft several times, the last time with extra stage directions that call for her to puzzle over the definition after Hero kisses her. Sale is indicating that what she feels after being kissed has left her confused, which Pynchon's outline and draft also say she is, but her puzzling over the sociological definition of "love" would be uncharacteristic, particularly because she shouldn't be able to connect her feelings to the idea of love—the concept of which is foreign to her despite her believing she understands the definition—until much later. That inability should remain even after Hero sings what Pynchon calls a "love song" in his outline, the available draft of which, written in Sale's hand, was unlikely to be acceptable, because it shows Broad's being aware of what would make her fall in love. The song is a duet in which Hero and Broad describe the type of girl and guy they "like" for several verses and finally describe "love" in the last verse of each singer's part. Broad, however, isn't ready to use the word "love" as far into the play as Sale's Act 3, scene 1, not doing so until the end of Pynchon's outline of Act 3, scene 2. How could she think of using the word in the second scene of the first act or know the type of guy she loves? Pynchon does not completely ignore Sale, relegating the possibility that Broad puzzles over the idea of love to a stage direction, which notes, "She is fascinated, but love? Maybe. Hero goes off, Broad puzzled. She consults the machine" (Act 1, scene 2). Without dialogue in which Broad comments on her puzzlement, an audience would not know what she is thinking about, and Pynchon's "Maybe" could be either a question for Sale, a note about the play rather than a part of the stage direction, or a concise reworking of the line "we aren't certain its anything like love" (Act 1, scene 2) in Sale's stage directions. Her consulting the machine without speaking, as Pynchon's draft has it, would leave the audience wondering what she is looking for, much as she could be wondering about what she feels.

80   In Sale's version, Ivy/Broad is that "fool woman machine," and Prostitute says she "detected a little something in that girl, something a touch different from the rest of those goddam zombies" (Act 1, scene 1). The "touch different" isn't exactly correct, as Tube Tester's interest in Whore and the presence of the pregnant woman (Act 1, scene 3) illustrate.

81   Keeping the carnival remnants would be necessary, not simply a good idea, if Johnny Badass's plan were thwarted. Sale, it

is true, is making a different point here, explaining that although the unmaterialistic minstrels "simply do not care enough about such physical, unimportant things," their unimportance does not take away from their superficial usefulness as scenery. Those remnants, however, serve as a symbol of the island's survival as a space removed from the IBM world, and the minstrels care enough to defend the carnival booth, the one remnant that Broad and her crew attempt to remove. The physical presence of the remnants, then, is important. Sale is not thinking about the larger implications of the idea that is helping him make his point. Indeed, the contrast between the minstrels and the IBMers does not seem to be a contrast between spiritualism and materialism, as Sale is implying, but rather between a brand of Romantic ideology that mingles spiritualism with a non-capitalistic materialism and a corporate ideology, though Sale doesn't seem completely at home with that brand of Romanticism, something evinced by his describing Whore and Tube Tester as "a little too low class to think about the problems that have faced the two thinkers," Hero and Broad (Act 3, scene 1). That is exactly the kind of elitism the minstrels are resisting, akin to Broad's calling them "[y]ou poor backward creatures"—or in Sale's version "you poor backward people" (Act 1, scene 1)—and noting, "[i]f you only realized how much you need the benefits our civilization will bring you" (P Act 1, scene 1).

82   For Pynchon's later use of the idea that love is a subversive force and his drawing on Orwell to work it into his fiction, see note 35 above.

83   The rendering of the sentence by using initials in this letter to Sale demonstrates that Pynchon's friends had heard or read the same words numerous times.

84   The second letter is signed Roscoe Stein, a name that Charles Hollander is surely right to consider "a typographical error" (46). Hollander nevertheless goes on to treat "Roscoe" as a reference to the nineteenth-century New York senator Roscoe Conkling, whose name appears twice in *Against the Day* (2006), and calls the name "a very subtle, well camouflaged, and cleverly set up half-name allusion" (47). The signature Roscoe is either a choice or an error, its appearance, if an error, perhaps explaining the use of Bosc. as a signature in the remaining articles. For the risk of mistakenly turning Bosc. into Rosc., while preparing the pages for typesetting, would be lower.

85   For a video of one of the commercials, see "Give Chocolate Syrup to Your Hyperactive Kids for Better Health!" John Edgar Wideman, in his novel *Hurry Home* (1970), makes an explicit

connection between El Bosco and the chocolate syrup Bosco, calling El Bosco "the ridiculous Spanish title bestowed on [Hieronymus Bosch . . .] with its association of chocolate milk, cookies, and talking cows," and writing that the association "did nothing to dispel the foglike gloom [from the mind of the novel's main character, Cecil Braithwaite] that seemed to seep from within [Bosch's] canvases" (52). The association is anachronistic; the title El Bosco, already established by the nineteenth century, predates the appearance of the syrup.

    86   The first syllable of Faggiaducci's name suggests a passing knowledge of Freud's view.

    87   *Yankee Doodle Dandy* suggests a connection between the pride sung about in "Harrigan" and Cohan's own personal pride, which, the movie also suggests, is related to Cohan's early development as a writer and entertainer, so inaccurately placing the composition of "Harrigan" before Cohan's success makes thematic sense.

    88   Herman's seeing in the pieces an opportunity for "fellow pupils to make connections with elements from their own school environment" ("Early Pynchon" 20)—a game given away, Herman goes on to write, by the implied correspondence between the fictional and the nonfictional groups The Boys—suggests that a Pynchon surrogate can be found among Hamster High's population.

    89   Wallace may also have been consciously using the space in the copyright page to relegate the idea of Pynchon's influence on his work to the margins, implicitly, if disingenuously, comparing our potential perception of its presence in *Infinite Jest* to Romain Gary's perception of his own work in *The Crying of Lot 49*. Wallace was certainly bothered by the emphasis placed on what he owed to Pynchon, seemingly because of the reception of his clearly *Lot-49*-influenced first novel, *The Broom of the System* (1986). He went out of his way, sometimes unbidden and thus counterproductively, to deflect attention from Pynchon's influence. On a radio appearance during his promotional tour for *Infinite Jest*, for example, he begins answering a listener's question about his use of dialogue in *Broom* by observing, "It was hard when that book came out because the Japanese lady from *The New York Times* and other people said it was a rip-off of *The Crying of Lot 49*, which in my own defense *I claim* I had not read at that time" (Jasty; emphasis mine). He then goes on to discuss other influences on the book, those that had gone unrecognized and that are related to his use of dialogue. Mentioning Pynchon was unnecessary. Similarly, he needlessly denies a Pynchon connection when he responds to Zachary Chouteau's question, during a 1997

interview for the American Booksellers Association, about whose fiction his writing might be compared to: "The Pynchon thing really annoys me. I haven't read him for so long. I get tired of it, pissed off by it." Later that year, during an appearance on NPR's *Weekend Sunday,* he could not even bring himself to say Pynchon's name and yet obliged his listeners to think about it: "I bristle sometimes at getting compared to some older—like some of these classic postmodern guys. The—the—the 'P' guy comes into mind. I won't even say his name. [...] And nothing against him. I just—I think he's got a very large kind of scientifically-based conception of the universe. And it's real interesting. [...] I think whatever I'm interested in, it's much more having to do with people, which sounds very trite" (see Vitale).

Surely Wallace's denials are evidence of what Harold Bloom, the critic whose studies Wallace denounces as "stupefyingly turgid-sounding shit" (*IJ* 911), calls the "anxiety of influence," an "aesthetic consciousness . . . denying obligation" (Bloom 6) as its possessor moves beyond the precursor and fashions his own voice. As Bloom observes, "Weaker talents idealize; figures of capable imagination appropriate for themselves" (5). While writing *Infinite Jest,* Wallace did successfully accomplish such an emancipatory appropriation from Pynchon's fiction—as well as from that of others, among them Don DeLillo and William Gaddis, whose influence did not seem to so powerfully threaten Wallace's sense of distinctiveness. He "burned off the annoying Pynchonesque echoes of his 1986 debut novel," as Michiko Kakutani puts it, and, in the process, transformed that which was Pynchonesque in his work into something that was his own. Still, as Bloom asks, "what strong maker desires the realization that he has failed to create himself?" (5). So Wallace asserts his originality and counters the accusation that he has merely ripped Pynchon off by simultaneously marginalizing Pynchon and appropriating Pynchon's own defense against an accusation of ripping off another writer. *Infinite Jest* is thus partially framed by the repudiation of Pynchon's influence. (For the affinities between *Infinite Jest* and Pynchon's work, see Sven Birkerts and Marshall Boswell.)

90   Of course, Pynchon may simply have been inclined to assent to the criticism, mulling it over as he figured out what kind of novelist he hoped to become and then ultimately rejecting it. When Smith read *The Crying of Lot 49,* he found fault with its conventionality. "I wrote saying I was a little disappointed. Perhaps I was spoiled," Smith told Dudar. "It was a conventional novel and I was looking for more than that. He wrote back and said he was inclined to agree"

(36). Pynchon may have been thinking of Smith's criticism when, in a July 1, 1970, letter to him, he worried "that the novel [which became *Gravity's Rainbow*] 'could be the biggest piece of shit since *The Crying of Lot 49*'" (quoted in Howard).

91   The comment to Shetzline and Beal suggests that Pynchon's thanking Bruce Allen for his "extravagant review of *Gravity's Rainbow*" was not entirely frank, particularly because Pynchon goes on to say, "It was a good ego trip for me" (March 25, 1973). He characterizes "an ego trip" in negative terms elsewhere (see To Arthur Mizener, November 25, 1970), and in the Allen letter, he also notes that the review "must've cheered up Viking's advertising people," a concern that the remainder of the letter shows was not a top priority for him.

92   David Letzler has recently written about the inaccuracies in Pynchon's undergraduate understanding of entropy, demonstrating the honesty of Pynchon's confession in *Slow Learner* that it was shallow (13). Letzler points out, among other things, that Saul is wrong to treat the terms "ambiguity," "redundance," "irrelevance," and "leakage" as different manifestations of noise in Information Theory and objects to the tendency of critics to accept Saul's mistake for fact (see 33–34), although Letzler inaccurately describes Saul's treatment of the terms, including "noise," as synonymous, or to be exact and address Letzler's dismissal of my description (2017) in his response to my critique in *Orbit*, as nearly synonymous. That is not, in fact, how Saul treats the concepts. Saul treats the first four terms as subcategories of noise, which is not the same thing as being nearly synonymous. "Rat" and "squirrel" belong to the category "rodent" but are not synonymous, even nearly so. (To be fair to Letzler, he too treats the terms as subcategories when he turns to his discussion of how they are used in the story; the problem with the way he introduces the issue is a diction problem.) That doesn't make Saul correct. For Information Theorists, the terms are not necessarily subsumed by the category noise. One can, for instance, "introduce redundancy properly so as to overcome the effects of noise" (Shannon 261) rather than create noise.

Readers, nonetheless, have little choice but to accept Saul's explanation in the context of "Entropy," because that is the story's understanding of the terms. To reject it is to make the story uninterpretable, or to deny the reader the ability to see how the parts work together. The story, of course, should not be used to teach how the concepts should be understood in Information Theory or to introduce students to entropy, and Letzler does a service to English professors who might otherwise not fact check the characters. Having acknowledged that Saul does not accurately understand Information Theory, critics will still want to understand what "Entropy" is up to, something that requires the reader to take Saul at his word, unless one is to argue that the story's shallow understanding of Information Theory and entropy renders the elements of it that are dependent on that understanding worthless to Pynchon's construction of the story or undermines its value as a manifestation of Pynchon's aesthetic development.

Letzler goes on to address the related issue of the supposed meaninglessness of Saul's discussion of the phrase "I love you" in the context of Information Theory. Saul discusses the complication of saying "I love you" as a problem of noise, apparently treating "redundancy" and "ambiguity" as the applicable subcategories, as Letzler's analysis demonstrates (34–35). The two other terms in Saul's list do not seem relevant to Saul's discussion. They thereby represent noise, and that's "[h]alf of what [he] just said" (91), we might note, appropriating Saul's own line. Saul's adding the two extra terms thus seems a subtle use of Pynchon's "misattribution of [Claude E. Shannon's] 50 percent figure to noise instead of redundancy" (Letzler 35), an error in "Entropy" that illustrates that Pynchon must have learned about Shannon's talk from a secondhand source, something also suggested by his not being aware of the mathematician Leonard J. Savage's demonstration, during Shannon's talk, of the value of redundancy when it comes to a husband's saying "I love you" to his wife throughout a marriage (Letzler 35).

In the context of Pynchon's thought, however, Saul's discourse on "I love you" does have meaning. First, it relates, in terms of its ambiguity, to the double quality of Pynchon's thinking about love at the time, that is, his seeing it as an affirmation of life (see To Sale and Mahool, c. January 1959) and as a negation of life through its association with death (see *SL* 5), a contradiction that could render the term meaningless as an idea, if not as a definable word. The possible doubleness may not be immediately apparent in Saul's discussion but may have influenced Pynchon's choice of the 37° temperature, a temperature that is as warm as life on the Celsius scale and as cold as death on the Fahrenheit scale. "Cute, huh?" (*SL* 13). Redundancy, meanwhile, has remained problematic for Pynchon. One thinks of Doc's "footnote that the word ["love"] these days was being way overused" (*IV* 5) so that it was losing its meaning. That's not to say that Pynchon's understanding wasn't shallow; it is to say that the shallowness enabled Pynchon to appropriate elements of Information Theory and use them in ways that make sense in the context of his

The Demon in the Text   135

thought, if not in the context of the thought of the theorists from whom he believed he was borrowing.

Similarly, the way the lack of soundness to "Pynchon's treatment of thermodynamic entropy" (Letzler 36) manifests itself could very well be the result of Pynchon's treating contexts that would not normally overlap as if they did so, that is, his trying to make sense of concepts taken from thermodynamics without his doing the necessary work to learn the field and thus employing them in ways they are used in a different context. In the case of the idea of chaos, that other context is Classical elemental thought, a discussion of which would have been standard in 1950s courses in both Classical and English Renaissance Literature, in which latter the use of death as a metaphor for orgasm or love making would have also been discussed. The elemental cosmos appears to be alluded to in the description of the changing weather pattern: "Outside there was rain. [. . .] The day before, it had snowed and the day before that there had been winds of gale force and before that the sun had made the city glitter" (82). We have, if you like, water, earth, wind, and fire. ("Snow," as Paracelsus explained, was made up of "crystals and beryls," and under the right conditions "the water which is in combination with the snow is coagulated into a stone" [225]. Note that water, as is explained here, is not only distinct from the snow but also transformed into stone by it, making the snow a manifestation of the element of earth, that is, all stone.) There are two notions of chaos in this system of thought, a pre-creation notion as an undifferentiated mass, that is, chaos as it was when the elements had yet to become distinct from each other, and a post-creation notion, that is, chaos as it is when it returns and one of the elements comes to dominate so much that the others cease to be manifest. The story of the Flood, for example, is a story of a return to chaos: water predominates. Similarly, Ovid's description of Andromeda when Perseus finds her chained to a rock (*Metamorphoses* Book IV) draws on the notion of chaos's return at the level of the individual: in her story, earth predominates. "Andromeda bound to the stone is, in effect," as Leonard Barkan puts it, "transformed into stone" (53): she is petrified. Post-creation chaos can thus seem disordered, as it does during the Flood, or static, as it does in the statuesque figure of Andromeda.

The paradox of the latter manifestation of chaos is that it is chaos as a homogeneous state, that is, a state in which everything is transmuted into one element: into earth, into wind, into fire, or into water. The genius of Pynchon's running through the weird changes in the weather is that on a meta-level there is, as is the case of the temperature, no meaningful change, because each condition symbolizes the same thing, a manifestation of chaos as homogeneity, but taken together they seem to signify chaos in the sense it is used in standard English, that is, as something synonymous with disorder. The changing weather that symbolizes sameness thus appears as the wildness one imagines when trying to conceive of pre-creation chaos, even though pre-creation chaos is also homogeneous, because it lacks differentiation. The pre-modern elemental cosmos, of course, has very little in common with the thermodynamic cosmos, but the notion of entropy participates in the same paradox as the Classical notion of chaos, that is, it envisions a chaotic state that is also a homogeneous one. Pynchon's understanding of entropy, both thermodynamic and informational, may have been misguided, but his ability to work with what he thought he knew was as magical as anything Paracelsus would have liked to perform with his knowledge.

93   I am using the concept of centropy, which seems to have been taken up in mystical texts more than in scientific texts since it was coined, as defined in Irving Simon's *Centropy: The Vertical Aspect of Evolution* (1980). Simon, resolving to use a more positive alternative to the term "negentropy," writes, "Centropy comes from the term 'centration,' which has been introduced by J. Sam Bois to indicate what happens when there is a pooling of human energies. It is a concentration of a sort; a uniting as exemplified by a group engaged in a cooperative venture. It is at those times when humans commingle (share in a common endeavor), that the outgrowth of their interaction may result in a new innovation leading to the enhancement of human relationships. Just such events occurred when single-celled organisms joined together to form multicellular organisms, and when complex organisms joined to form larger structures such as societies."

Bibliography

Alexander, Paul. *Salinger: A Biography.* New York: Macmillan, 2000.
Anderson, Paul Thomas. *Inherent Vice.* Burbank, CA: Warner Brothers, 2014.
———. *Inherent Vice*: Screenplay. Burbank, CA: Warner Brothers, 2013: http://pdl.warnerbros.com/wbmovies/awards2014/pdf/iv.pdf.
Arthur, Rosemary A. *Pseudo-Dionysius as Polemicist.* Aldershot, UK: Ashgate, 2008.
Barkan, Leonard. *The Gods Made Flesh: Metamorphosis and the Pursuit of Paganism.* New Haven: Yale University Press, 1986.
Barthes, Roland. *Camera Lucida: Reflections on Photography.* Trans. Richard Howard. New York: Hill and Wang, 1981.
Batchelor, John Calvin. "Thomas Pynchon Is Not Thomas Pynchon." *Soho Weekly News* (April 22–28, 1976), 15–17, 21, 35.
———. "The Ghost of Richard Fariña." *Soho Weekly News* (April 28–May 4, 1977), 19–22, 26–27.
Bell, Bill. "A Blessing in Disguise: Ghoul Fest at Cathedral Raises the Dread." *Daily News* (October 30, 1996): articles.nydailynews.com/1996-10-30/entertainment/18012060_1_largest-cathedral-dr-caligari-silent-film, accessed August 12, 2012.
"Between Issues." *The New Leader* 48:9 (April 26, 1965), 2.
Birkerts, Sven. "The Alchemist's Retort: A Multi-Layered Postmodern Saga of Damnation and Salvation." *Atlantic Monthly* 277:2 (February 1996), 106–113.
Bloom, Harold. *The Anxiety of Influence: A Theory of Poetry.* Oxford: Oxford University Press, 1975 [1973].

Blum, Richard H. *Society and Drugs*, Vol. I. San Francisco: Jossey-Bass, 1970.
Blumenthal, John. "How I Got Thomas Pynchon's Medical Records": https://www.goodreads.com/author_blog_posts/5792001-how-i-got-thomas-pynchon-s-medical-records, accessed May 17, 2017.
Boddy, Kasia. *The American Short Story Since 1950*. Edinburgh: Edinburgh University Press, 2010.
Bodroghkozy, Aniko. *Groove Tube: Sixties Television and The Youth Rebellion*. Durham: Duke University Press, 2001.
Bone, James. "Mystery Writer." *Times Magazine [London]* (June 14, 1997), 26–29. Academic OneFile, accessed February 15, 2016.
Boswell, Marshall. *Understanding David Foster Wallace*. Columbia: University of South Carolina Press, 2003.
Brown, Norman. O. *Love's Body*. Berkeley: University of California Press, 1990 [1966].
Buckley, William F. *Firing Line*. WOR-TV, September 3, 1968.
Burgess, Anthony. "The Art of Fiction No. 48." Interviewed by John Cullinan. *Paris Review* 56 (Spring 1973): https://www.theparisreview.org/interviews/3994/anthony-burgess-the-art-of-fiction-no-48-anthony-burgess, accessed May 9, 2017.
Burke, Tom. "Princess Leda's Castle in the Air." *Burke's Steerage*. New York: Putnam, 1976, 299–314.
Chouteau, Zachary. "Words with the Singular David Foster Wallace": rpt. http://www.smallbytes.net/~bobkat/aba.html, accessed November 25, 2016.
Cowart, David. *Thomas Pynchon & the Dark Passages of History*. Athens: University of Georgia Press, 2011.
Curtin, Michael and Lynn Spigel. *The Revolution Wasn't Televised: Sixties Television and Social Conflict*. New York: Routledge, 1997.
Daly, Kyle. "Maybe Thomas Pynchon Wasn't in *Inherent Vice* After All." *A.V. Club* (June 4, 2015): http://www.avclub.

com/article/maybe-thomas-pynchon-wasnt-inherent-vice-after-all-220352, accessed November 5, 2015.

Daugherty, Tracy. *Just One Catch: A Biography of Joseph Heller.* New York: St. Martin's Press, 2011.

"Diatribe of a Mad Housewife." *The Simpsons.* Created by Matt Groening. FOX Television, January 25, 2004.

Diebold, John and Michael Goodwin. Introduction. *Babies of Wackiness: A Readers' Guide to Thomas Pynchon's* Vineland: www.mindspring.com/~shadow88/intro.htm, accessed September 5, 2012.

Dubini, Donatello and Fosco. *Journey into the Mind of [P.].* West Long Branch, NJ: Kultur, 2008 [2002].

Dudar, Helen. "Lifting the Veil on Life of a Literary Recluse." *Chicago Tribune Bookworld* (April 8, 1984), 35–36: http://archives.chicagotribune.com/1984/04/08/page/407/article/lifting-the-veil-on-life-of-a-literary-recluse/index.html, accessed May 17, 2017.

Edmonds III, Radcliffe G. *Myths of the Underworld Journey: Plato, Aristophanes, and the "Orphic" Gold Tablets.* Cambridge, UK: Cambridge University Press, 2004.

Edmunds, Lowell. "Aristophanes' Acharnians." *Aristophanes: Essays in Interpretation.* Ed. Jeffrey Henderson. Cambridge, UK: Cambridge University Press, 1980: 1–42.

Feiffer, Jules. *Sick, Sick, Sick: A Guide to Non-Confident Living.* New York: McGraw-Hill, 1958.

Foley, Martha, ed. *Best American Short Stories and the Yearbook of the American Short Story, 1962.* Boston: Houghton Mifflin Company, 1962.

Foley, Martha, and David Burnett, eds. *Best American Short Stories and the Yearbook of the American Short Story, 1960.* Boston: Houghton Mifflin Company, 1960.

———. *Best American Short Stories and the Yearbook of the American Short Story, 1961.* Boston: Houghton Mifflin Company, 1961.

Foster, Graham. "Object of the Week: Pynchonalia." International Anthony Burgess Foundation (May 8,

2017): https://www.anthonyburgess.org/object-of-the-week/object-week-pynchonalia/, accessed May 9, 2017.

Freer, Joanna. *Thomas Pynchon and American Counterculture.* New York: Cambridge University Press, 2014.

Freud, Sigmund. *General Psychological Theory: Papers on Metapsychology.* Intro. by Philip Rieff. New York: Simon and Schuster, 1997.

Galvin, Kevin. "The Enigma of the Elusive Writer Thomas Pynchon." *Philadelphia Inquirer* (November 27, 1989), 8-D.

Ganz, Earl. "Pynchon in Hiding." *Plum* 3 (1980), 5–20.

Gibbs, Rodney. "A Portrait of the Luddite as a Young Man." *Denver Quarterly* 39.1 (2004), 35–42.

Ginsberg, Allen. "Howl." *Collected Poems, 1947–1980.* New York: Harper and Row, 1988, 126–33.

"Give Chocolate Syrup to Your Hyperactive Kids for Better Health!." *Michael's TV Tray* (March 15, 2013): https://michaelstvtray.com/2013/03/15/give-chocolate-syrup-to-your-hyperactive-kids-for/.

Glassow, Jonathan. Email Interview with Norman England (April 13, 2013). (Privately emailed to me).

Goolrick, Robert. "Pieces of Pynchon." *New Times* (October 16, 1978), 58–70: rpt. http://americanfiction.wordpress.com/2009/06/16/robert-goolrick-pieces-of-pynchon/, accessed January 4, 2012.

Gordon, Andrew. "Smoking Dope with Thomas Pynchon: A Sixties Memoir." *The Vineland Papers: Critical Takes on Pynchon's Novel.* Ed. Geoffrey Green et al. Normal, IL: Dalkey Archive Press, 1994, 167–78: rpt. http://users.clas.ufl.edu/agordon/pynchon.htm, accessed March 12, 2016.

Graf, Fritz and Sarah Iles Johnston. *Ritual Texts for the Afterlife: Orpheus and the Bacchic Gold Tablets,* 2nd ed. New York: Routledge, 2013.

Grant, J. Kerry. *A Companion to* V. Athens, GA: The University of Georgia Press, 2001.

Gratz, Roberta Brandes. *The Battle for Gotham: New York in the Shadow of Robert Moses and Jane Jacobs*. New York: Nation Books, 2010.
Green, Jonathon. *Cassell's Dictionary of Slang*. London: Weidenfeld and Nicolson, 2005.
Hajdu, David. *Positively 4th Street: The Lives and Times of Joan Baez, Bob Dylan, Mimi Baez Fariña and Richard Farina*. New York: Farrar, Straus & Giroux, 2001.
Hartnett, Michael. "A High School Record for Disturbing the Peace." *Pynchon Notes* 20–21 (1987), 115–20. DOI: http://doi.org/10.16995/pn.340.
Hayles, N. Katherine. "'Who Was Saved?': Families, Snitches, and Recuperation in Pynchon's Vineland." *The Vineland Papers: Critical Takes on Pynchon's Novel*. Ed. Geoffrey Green et al. Normal, IL: Dalkey Archive Press, 1994, 14–30.
Herman, Luc. "Early Pynchon." *The Cambridge Companion to Thomas Pynchon*. Ed. Inger H. Dalsgaard et al. Cambridge, UK: Cambridge University Press, 2012, 19–29.
Herman, Luc, and John M. Krafft. "From the Ground Up: The Evolution of the South-West Africa Chapter in Pynchon's *V*." *Contemporary Literature* 47:2 (2006), 261–288.
———. "Fast Learner: The Typescript of Pynchon's *V.* at the Harry Ransom Center in Austin." *Texas Studies in Literature and Language* 49:1 (2007), 1–20.
Herman, Luc, John M. Krafft, and Sharon B. Krafft. "Missing Link: The *V.* Galleys at the Morgan Library and the Harry Ransom Center." *Variants* 7 (2008), 139–157.
Herman, Luc, and Steven C. Weisenburger. *Gravity's Rainbow, Domination, and Freedom*. Athens: University of Georgia Press, 2013.
Hill, Robert R. "Decoding Community in Pynchon's *Vineland*: Problematic Definitions for Readers and Characters." *Pynchon Notes* 40–41 (1997): 197–217. DOI: http://doi.org/10.16995/pn.340.

Hitchens, Christopher. "American Notes." *Times Literary Supplement* (July 12, 1985), 772.
Hollander, Charles. "Pynchon's Juvenilia and *Against the Day*." *GRAAT* 3 (2008), 38–55.
Howard, Gerald. "From A to V." *BookForum* (Summer 2005): http://www.bookforum.com/archive/sum_05/pynchon.html, accessed August 11, 2012.
Hudes, Karen. "Epic Agent: The Great Candida Donadio." *Tin House* 6:4 (2005): 149–68.
Hurley, Patrick. *Pynchon Character Names: A Dictionary*. Jefferson, NC: McFarland, 2008.
Jasty, Kunal. "A Lost 1996 Interview with David Foster Wallace": https://medium.com/@kunaljasty/a-lost-1996-interview-with-david-foster-wallace-63987d93c2c#.zgcrt7977, accessed November 25, 2016.
Jay, Martin. "Abjection Overruled." *Salmagundi* 103 (1994), 235–51: http://0-literature.proquest.com.fama.us.es/searchFulltext.do?id=R01512017&divLevel=0&area=abell&forward=critref_ft, accessed March 23, 2016.
"Josh Brolin Interview, *Inherent Vice*." *Moviesaddicts.com* (January 12, 2015): http://moviesaddicts.com/interviews/josh-brolin-interview-inherent-vice/, accessed November 05, 2013.
Kachka, Boris. "P." *New York* (September 2–9, 2013), 46–52, 152–58. Rpt. as "On the Thomas Pynchon Trail: From the Long Island of His Boyhood to the 'Yupper West Side' of His New Novel": http://www.vulture.com/2013/08/thomas-pynchon-bleeding-edge.html, accessed May 18, 2017.
Kakutani, Michiko. "A Country Dying of Laughter. In 1,079 Pages." *New York Times* (February 13, 1996): http://www.nytimes.com/1996/02/13/books/books-of-the-times-a-country-dying-of-laughter-in-1079-pages.html, accessed, November 26, 2016.
Kellogg, Carolyn. "When Thomas Pynchon is Just Tom: A Remarkable Collection Debuts." *Los Angeles Times* (May 5, 2011): http://latimesblogs.latimes.

com/jacketcopy/2011/05/thomas-pynchon-tom-a-remarkable collection.html, accessed April 20, 2013.
Ken Lopez's Catalogue 135: lopezbooks.com/catalog/135/static/?page=8&refp=3, accessed August 12, 2012.
Ken Lopez's Catalogue 139: lopezbooks.com/catalog/139/static/?page=4&refp=2, accessed August 12, 2012.
Konstantinou, Lee. *Cool Characters: Irony and American Fiction.* Cambridge, MA: Harvard University Press, 2016.
Krafft, John. "Biographical Note." *The Cambridge Companion to Thomas Pynchon.* Ed. Inger H. Dalsgaard et al. Cambridge, UK: Cambridge University Press, 2012, 9–16.
"L. I. Aide Concedes Possible Padding." *New York Times* (October 8, 1963), 45.
Letzler, David. Crossed-Up Disciplinarity: What Norbert Wiener, Thomas Pynchon, and William Gaddis Got Wrong about Entropy and Literature." *Contemporary Literature* 56:1 (2015), 23–55.
———. "Response to Albert Rolls, and a Brief Institutional History of Literary Hermeneutics." *Orbit: A Journal of American Literature.* 5:2 (2017). DOI: http://doi.org/10.16995/orbit.222.
Malpas, Simon, and Andrew Taylor. *Thomas Pynchon.* Manchester: Manchester University Press, 2013.
Martin, Justin. "Ex-Oyster Bay Chief Who Knew T.R. Dies." *Newsday* [Nassau and Suffolk ed.] (July 23, 1995), A10.
Maschler, Tom. *Publisher.* London: Picador, 2005.
Max. D. T. *Every Love Story Is a Ghost Story: A Life of David Foster Wallace.* New York: Viking, 2012.
McClintock, Scott. "The Origins of the Family, Private Property, and the State of California in Pynchon's Fiction." *Pynchon's California.* Ed. Scott McClintock and John Miller. Iowa City: University of Iowa Press, 2014, 91–112.
McHale, Brian. *Constructing Postmodernism.* London: Routledge, 1992.

McLellan, Joseph. "Thomas Pynchon: A Short Mystery." *Washington Post Bookworld* (March 11, 1973), 2.

Meindl, Dieter. *American Fiction and the Metaphysics of the Grotesque.* Columbia: University of Missouri Press, 1996.

Menand, Louis. "Drive, He Wrote: What the Beats were about." *The New Yorker* (October 1, 2007): http://www.newyorker.com/magazine/2007/10/01/drive-he-wrote, accessed September 7, 2015.

Milton, John. *Paradise Lost.* Ed. Merritt Y. Hughes. New York: Odyssey Press, 1962.

Nassau County, Long Island, New York: https://lrv.nassaucountyny.gov/map/?s=25&b=56&l=35, accessed June 13, 2017.

"Newcomer." *John Larroquette Show.* Created by Don Reo. NBC, December 7, 1993.

Nichols, Lewis. "In and Out of Books." *New York Times Book Review* (April 28, 1963), 28.

Nietzsche, Friedrich. *The Birth of Tragedy and The Case of Wagner.* Trans. Walter Kaufmann. New York: Random House, 1967.

Ochester, Edwin. "*New World Writing 16*: Meaty Collection." *Cornell Daily Sun* (May 25, 1960): http://cdsun.library.cornell.edu/cgi-bin/cornell?a=d&d=CDS19600525-01.2.23&e=--------20--1-----all----, accessed May 5, 2017.

Otto, Walter F. *Dionysus: Myth and Cult.* Trans. and Intro. Robert B. Palmer. Bloomington: Indiana University Press, 1965.

Ovid. *Metamorphoses.* Trans. Rolfe Humphries. Bloomington: Indiana University Press, 1955.

Paracelsus, *Hermetic Chemistry: Volume 1 of The Hermetic and Alchemical Writings of Aureolus Philippus Theophrastus Bombast, of Hohenheim, Called Paracelsus the Great.* Trans. Arthur Edward Waite. London: J. Elliott, 1894.

Parker, James. "Review of *Inherent Vice.*" Barnes&-NobleReview.com (August 4, 2009): http://bnreview.barnesandnoble.com/t5/Reviews-Essays/Inherent-Vice/ba-p/1219, accessed April 6, 2013.

Patell, Cyrus R. K. *Negative Liberties: Morrison, Pynchon, and the Problem of Liberal Ideology.* Durham: Duke University Press, 2001.

Paz. "Blessing of the Animals 2011." (2011). *Paz's New York Minute*: http://www.pazsnewyorkminute.com/2011/10/blessing-of-the-animals-2011/, accessed August 12, 2012.

Plato. *The Collected Dialogues of Plato: Including the Letters.* Ed. Edith Hamilton and Huntington Cairns. Princeton: Princeton University Press, 1961.

Portinari, Natália. "The Fake Hermit." *Piauí* (May 2017): http://piaui.folha.uol.com.br/materia/the-fake-hermit, acessed June 25, 2017.

Porush, David. "'Purring into Trancendence': Pynchon's Puncutron Machine." *The Vineland Papers: Critical Takes on Pynchon's Novel.* Ed. Geoffrey Green et al. Normal, IL: Dalkey Archive Press, 1994, 31–45.

"Pynchon Chosen for Post as Oyster Bay Supervisor." *New York Times* (December 5, 1962), 53.

Pynchon, Thomas. "Juvenilia." (1952–1953). *Thomas Pynchon: A Bibliography of Primary and Secondary Materials.* Clifford Mead. Elmwood Park, IL: Dalkey Archive Press, 1989, 155–67.

——. To Kirkpatrick Sale and Patricia Mahool. c. January 1959. Harry Ransom Humanities Research Center, The University of Texas at Austin.

——. To Corlies Smith, August 31, 1961, *Of a Fond Ghoul.* New York: The Blown Litter Press, 1990.

——. To Corlies Smith, October 15, 1961, *Of a Fond Ghoul.* New York: The Blown Litter Press, 1990.

——. To Candida Donadio. November 2, 1961. Joseph Heller Collection, Brandeis University.

——. To Corlies Smith. March 13, 1962. *Of a Fond Ghoul.* New York: The Blown Litter Press, 1990.

——. To Corlies Smith. March 24, 1962. *Of a Fond Ghoul.* New York: The Blown Litter Press, 1990.

———. To Corlies Smith. April 19, 1962. *Of a Fond Ghoul.* New York: The Blown Litter Press, 1990.

———. To Corlies Smith. April 30, 1962. *Of a Fond Ghoul.* New York: The Blown Litter Press, 1990.

———. To Kirkpatrick Sale. May 28, 1962. Harry Ransom Humanities Research Center, The University of Texas at Austin.

———. To Corlies Smith. June 2, 1962. *Of a Fond Ghoul.* New York: The Blown Litter Press, 1990.

———. To Faith Sale. October 1, 1962. Harry Ransom Humanities Research Center, The University of Texas at Austin.

———. To Bob Hillock. December 1, 1962. http://www.sothebys.com/en/auctions/ecatalogue/2017/fine-books-manuscripts-n09658/lot.248.html, accessed December 1, 2017

———. To Faith Sale. November 23, 1962. Harry Ransom Humanities Research Center, The University of Texas at Austin.

———. *V.* [ARC]. Philadelphia: J. B. Lippincott, 1963.

———. To Kirkpatrick and Faith Sale. March 9, 1963. Harry Ransom Humanities Research Center, The University of Texas at Austin.

———. To Faith and Kirkpatrick Sale. June 2, 1963. Harry Ransom Humanities Research Center, The University of Texas at Austin.

———. To Kirkpatrick and Faith Sale. June 29, 1963. Harry Ransom Humanities Research Center, The University of Texas at Austin.

———. *V.* London: Jonathan Cape, 1963.

———. To Kirkpatrick and Faith Sale. March 27, 1964. Harry Ransom Humanities Research Center, The University of Texas at Austin.

———. To Bob Hillock. April 11, 1964. http://www.sothebys.com/en/auctions/ecatalogue/2017/fine-books-manuscripts-n09658/lot.250.html, accessed December 1, 2017.

———. To Richard Fariña. October 16, 1965. Archival Collection, Random House Records, 1925-1999. Columbia University Libraries.

———. To Stanley Hyman. December 8, 1965. Stanley Edgar Hyman papers, 1932–1978, Library of Congress.

———. *The Crying of Lot 49*. Philadelphia: J. B. Lippincott Company, 1966.

———. "Journey into the Mind of Watts" *New York Times* (June 12, 1966), 264, 286–89.

———. "Pros and Cohns," *New York Times Book Review* (July 17, 1966), 22, 24.

———. To Arthur Mizener. November 25, 1970. Papers of Stephen M. Tomaske. The Huntington Library. (Photocopy).

———. *Gravity's Rainbow*. New York: Viking, 1973.

———. To Bruce Allen. March 25, 1973. http://thomaspynchon.com/thomas-pynchon-1973-letter-to-bruce-allen-and-the-marketing-of-gravitys-rainbow/, accessed June 10, 2017.

———. To David Shetzline and M. F. Beal, January 21, 1974. Papers of Stephen M. Tomaske. The Huntington Library. (Photocopy).

———. To a Young Novelist. May 21, 1978. Private Collection.

———. To Donald Barthelme. c. 1983. Donald Barthelme Literary Papers University of Houston, Special Collections.

———. Introduction. *Been Down So Long It Looks Like Up to Me*. By Richard Fariña. New York: Viking, 1983, vii–xviii.

———. Two Letters to Michael Stephens. c. 1983. https://www.betweenthecovers.com/pages/books/ 399032/thomas-pynchon/two-typed-letters-signed-about-the-possible-polish-translation-of-his-work, accessed August 25, 2017.

———. *Slow Learner*. Boston: Little, Brown and Company, 1984.

———. "Is It O.K. to Be a Luddite?" *New York Times Book Review* (October 28, 1984), 1, 40–41. Rpt. *New Media*. Ed. Albert Rolls. New York: H. W. Wilson, 169–75.

———. "The Heart's Eternal Vow." *New York Times* (April 10, 1988), Section 7:1: http://www.nytimes.com/books/98/12/06/specials/marquez-cholera.html.

———. *Vineland*. Boston: Little, Brown and Company, 1990.

———. Introduction. *The Teachings of Don B.: Satires, Parodies, Fables, Illustrated Stories, and Plays of Donald Barthelme*. Ed. Kim Herzinger. New York: Turtle Bay, 1992, xv–xxii.

———. *Mason & Dixon*. New York: Little Brown, 1997.

———. Introduction. *Stone Junction*. By Jim Dodge. New York: Grove Press, 1997, xi–xiv.

———. "Hallowe'en? Over Already?" *Cathedral School Newsletter*, January 1999, 1 and 3.

———. Foreword. *Nineteen Eighty-Four*. By Orwell, George. New York: Plume, 2003, vii–xxvi.

———. *Against the Day*. New York: Penguin Press, 2006.

———. *Inherent Vice*. New York: Penguin Press, 2009.

———. *Bleeding Edge*. New York: Penguin Press, 2013.

Pynchon, Thomas and Corlies Smith. *Of a Fond Ghoul: Being the Correspondence between Corlies M. Smith and Thomas Pynchon*. New York: The Blown Litter Press, 1990. (Photocopy of letters, without internal Lippincott memos, in Papers of Stephen M. Tomaske. The Huntington Library).

Pynchon, Thomas, and Kirkpatrick Sale. "Minstrel Island." 1958. Harry Ransom Humanities Research Center, The University of Texas at Austin.

Reese, Andrew. "An Addict's View of Drug Abuse." *Junkies and Straights: The Camarillo Experience*. Ed. Robert H. Coombs. Lexington, MA: Lexington Books, 1975, 5–19.

Rink, Deane. "Dialogue on favorite books with Deane Rink, Part 2." *B&R Samizdat Express* (Nov. 17, 1196): http://www.samizdat.com/rink2.html, accessed August 20, 2012.

Roeder, Bill. "After the Rainbow." *Newsweek* (August 7, 1978), 7.

Rollins, Peter C., ed. *The Columbia Companion to American History on Film*. New York: Columbia University Press, 2004.
Rolls, Albert. "Review of *Bleeding Edge*, by Thomas Pynchon." *Orbit: Writing around Pynchon* 2:1 (2013). DOI: http://doi.org/10.7766/orbit.v2.1.51, accessed July 14, 2015.
———. "Who's Afraid of the Big Bad Freak: Inherent Vice Comes to the Big Screen," *Berfrois* (October 21, 2014): http://www.berfrois.com/2014/10/inherent-vice-comes-to-the-big-screen-albert-rolls/, accessed July 14, 2015.
Royster, Paul. "Thomas Pynchon: A Brief Chronology," digitalcommons.unl.edu, accessed August 12, 2012.
Sales, Nancy Jo. "Meet Your Neighbor, Thomas Pynchon." *New York* (November 11, 1996), 60–64.
Schaap, Dick. "No Return Address on the V-Mail." *Book Week* (May 10, 1964), 6.
Schaub, Thomas. "Playing Bridge with Thomas Pynchon." *Thomas Pynchon: American Novelist* (September 7, 2017): http://thomaspynchon.com/author/thomas-schaub/, accessed September 12, 2017.
Seed, David. *The Fictional Labyrinths of Thomas Pynchon*. Iowa City: University of Iowa Press, 1988.
Shannon, Claude E. "The Redundancy of English." *Cybernetics: The Macy-Conferences 1946–1953*. Vol. 1: Transactions. Ed. Claus Pias. Zürich: Diaphanes, 2003, 248–72.
Siegel, Jules et al. *Lineland: Mortality and Mercy on the Internet's Pynchon-L@Waste.Org Discussion List*. Philadelphia: Intangible Assets Manufacturing, 1997.
Siegel, Jules. "Revolution." *Playboy* 17:3 (March 1970), 140, 185–93.
Silberman, James. To Thomas Pynchon. July 5, 1966. Archival Collection, Random House Records, 1925–1999. Columbia University Libraries.
Silliman, Ron. "Review *Journey into the Mind of [P.]*." Silliman's Blog (August 16, 2006): http://ronsilliman.blogspot.com/2006/08/danish-documentary-thomas-pynchon.html, accessed July 9, 2012.

Silverman, Al. *The Time of Their Lives: The Golden Age of Great American Publishers, Their Editors and Authors*. New York: St Martin's Press, 2008.

Simon, Irving. *Centropy: The Vertical Aspect of Evolution*. Bombay: D.A.I. Publishers, 1989 [1980]. Available at http://web.archive.org/web/20040419074009/http://irvingsimon.com:80/preface.htm, accessed September 10, 2017.

Sinkler, Rebecca. "The Gray Lady and the 'P' Word." *Columbia Journalism Review* 33:6 (March/April 1995), 69.

Siropoulos, Vagelis. "The Dionysian (Gay) Abject." Cited in José M. Yebra. "A Terrible Beauty." *Ethics and Trauma in Contemporary British Fiction*. Ed. Jean-Michel Ganteau. Amsterdam: Rodopi, 2011, 175–208.

Sontag, Susan. *Under the Sign of Saturn*. New York: Picador, 2002 [1980].

Staller, Karen M. *Runaways: How the Sixties Counterculture Shaped Today's Practices and Policies*. New York: Columbia University Press, 2006.

Standard Dictionary of Facts. Buffalo: Frontier Press Company, 1922.

Tanner, Tony. *Thomas Pynchon*. London: Methuen, 1982.

Terres, John K. *Songbirds in Your Garden*. Chapel Hill, NC: Algonquin Books, 1994.

"That Which Has Seemingly Influenced Thomas Pynchon" (nd): http://www.pynchon.pomona.edu/bio/influences.html, accessed October 12, 2015.

Thompson, Hunter S. "The Great Shark Hunt." *The Great Shark Hunt: Strange Tales from a Strange Time*. New York: Simon and Shuster, 2003 [1979], 421–52.

Tomaske, Stephen. "Notes Toward a Paper on the Ford Foundation Document." Papers of Stephen M. Tomaske: Circa 1989 The Huntington Library.

——. Interview with Corlies M. Smith, May 10 2001. Papers of Stephen M. Tomaske, The Huntington Library.

——. Interview with Harriet Wasserman, June 28, 2001. Papers of Stephen M. Tomaske, The Huntington Library.

———. Interview with Corlies M. Smith, August 3, 2001. Papers of Stephen M. Tomaske, The Huntington Library.

Trotter, J. K. "Thomas Pynchon Returns to New York, Where He's Always Been." (2013, June 17, 2013) *Atlantic Wire*: http://www.thewire.com/entertainment/2013/06/thomas-pynchon-back-new-york/66140/, accessed November 25, 2015.

Veggian, Henry. *Mercury of the Waves: Modern Cryptology and U.S. Literature.* Doctoral Dissertation, University of Pittsburgh, 2005: http://d-scholarship.pitt.edu/9870/1/HVDissertationETD.pdf, accessed November 28, 2013.

Vitale, Tom. *Weekend Sunday* (May 18, 1997): rpt. http://www.smallbytes.net/~bobkat/npr.html, accessed November 25, 2016.

Wales, Henry Basil, and Harry Owen Lathrop. *The Conservation of Natural Resources: A Textbook for Junior and Senior High Schools.* Chicago: Laurel Book Company, 1944.

Wallace, David Foster. *Infinite Jest.* New York: Back Bay Books, 2006 [1996].

———. "Borges on the Couch." *New York Times* (November 7, 2004): http://www.nytimes.com/2004/11/07/books/review/07WALLACE.html?_r=0, accessed March 12, 2016.

Ware, Tim. "Thomas Pynchon: American Novelist: Media." http://thomaspynchon.com/pynchon-media/, accessed June 6, 2016.

Warren Commission Report: Report of the President's Commission on the Assassination of President John F. Kennedy. New York: St Martin's Press, 1992.

Weisenburger, Steven C. "Thomas Pynchon at Twenty-Two: A Recovered Autobiographical Sketch." *American Literature* 62:4 (1990), 692–97.

———. *A* Gravity's Rainbow *Companiom*, 2nd ed. Athens: University of Georgia Press, 2006.

———. "Gravity's Rainbow." *The Cambridge Companion to Thomas Pynchon*, ed. Inger H. Dalsgaard et al. Cambridge, UK: Cambridge University Press, 2012, 44–58.

"Where's Thomas Pynchon?" CNN (June 5, 1997): http://cgi.cnn.com/US/9706/05/pynchon/, accessed October 10, 2013.

Wickman, Forrest. "Thomas Pynchon Will Cameo in *Inherent Vice*—but Will We Recognize Him?" *Slate* (September 26, 2014): http://www.slate.com/blogs/browbeat/2014/09/26/thomas_pynchon, accessed October 10, 2014.

Wideman, John Edgar. *Hurry Home*. New York: Harcourt, Brace & World, 1970.

Winston, Mathew. "The Quest for Pynchon." *Mindful Pleasures: Essays on Thomas Pynchon*. Ed. George Levine and David Leverenz. Boston: Little Brown and Company, 1976, 251–63.

Williams, Scott. "John Larroquette's Dark Ride ... Opposite Roseanne." Associated Press (March 7, 1994): http://w3.nexis.com/new/, accessed October 21, 2010.

Wisnicki, Adrian. "A Trove of New Works by Thomas Pynchon? *Bomarc Service News* Rediscovered." *Pynchon Notes* 46–49 (2001), 9–34. DOI: http://doi.org/10.16995/pn.88.

Yebra, José M. "'A Terrible Beauty': Ethics, Aesthetics, and the Trauma of Gayness in Alan Hollinghurst's *The Line of Beauty*." *Ethics and Trauma in Contemporary British Fiction*. Eds. Susana Onega and Jean-Michel Ganteau. Amsterdam: Rodopi, 2011, 175–208.

Index

Allen, Bruce 133 n91
American Library Association 103–4 n10
Anderson, Paul Thomas 7, 26, 37–38, 65, 119 n59, 121 n61
Apollonian 28, 30, 61, 63, 68, 69
Aptos 123 n71
Arcata 123 n71
authorial stand-ins 22–24, 68, 85, 109 n28, 121 n70
autobiography/life story 3, 7, 15–17, 21–24, 50, 69, 72, 108 n21, 109 n28, 114 n48, 123 n72

Badass 41, 48
Baez-Fariña, Mimi 5–6, 10, 97
Barkan, Leonard 135 n92
Barthelme, Donald 45–46, 90, 114 nn49 and 50, 123 n71; *Teachings of Don B.* 18, 40
Barthes, Roland 18, 24, 25, 108 n22
Batchelor, John Calvin 7, 102 n5, 106 n12
B&R Samizdat Express 3
Beal, Mary (M. F.) 34, 42, 43, 45–46, 89–90, 115 n51, 133 n91
Beats 23, 28, 31, 71, 73, 101–2 n4, 124 n74
Benjamin, Walter 24
Berkeley, 10, 113 n45
Bernstein, Leonard 14, 107 n19; *West Side Story* 14, 107 n19
Best American Short Stories 4, 101 n3
biography 3, 8, 9, 16, 18, 22, 23, 24, 50, 86, 91, 108 n23, 109 n27
Bloom, Harold 132 n89
Blum, Richard H. 110 n30
Boddy, Kasia 97
Bodroghkozy, Aniko 112 n39
Boeing 10, 21, 103 n9
Bomarc Service News 103 n9
Bonanza 55
Bone, James 8, 69
Bosch, Hieronymus 81, 131 n85
Bosco, 80–81, 130–31 n85
Brady Bunch 46, 118 n53
Brolin, Josh 7, 102 n6
Brown, Norman O. 110 n34
Buckley, William 28; *Firing Line* 28
Burgess, Anthony 21
Burke, Tom 112 n40

California 10, 31, 67, 68, 123 n71
Carver, Catherine 88, 89
Cathedral of Saint John the Divine 1–3, 6, 101 n1
Cathedral School 1, 102 n5
centropy 136 n93
Chouteau, Zachary 131 n89
Classicism/Classical 22, 69, 71, 88, 123–24 n73, 135 n92
CNN 13, 107 n17
Cohan, George M. 84–85, 131 n87
Conkling, Roscoe 130 n84
Connolly, Richard 115 n51
Cornell 3, 5–6, 10, 19, 56–57, 60, 91, 101–2 n4, 103–4 n10, 106 n12, 120 nn62–63
Cornell Daily Sun 101–2 n4
Cowart, David 40, 55, 114 n47
Curtin, Michael 55

Damascius 61
Darth Vader 3
Daugherty, Tracy 117 n52
Dean, Jimmy 126 n78
DeLillo, Don 132 n89
Derrida, Jacques 31–32
Deville, Willy 9
Dial 105–6 n12
DiCaprio, Leonardo 2
Diebold, John 5, 101 n4
Dionysian 27–30, 31, 41, 61, 63, 68, 69
Dionysius the Areopagite 27–28
Dionysus 27, 61
Dodge, Jim 48; *Stone Junction* 48, 49
Donadio, Candida 7, 11–12, 15, 21, 24, 43, 46, 103 n9, 104 n10, 105–6 n12, 116 n51, 116–17 n52, 122 n70
dreams 16–19
drugs 25–26, 27, 30, 33, 35, 39, 44, 102 n6, 11 n35. Types of: amphetamines 26, 33, 39; downers 26; heroin 31–33, 47, 53, 56, 66, 67, 82, 111 n35, 119 nn55, 59, and 60; LSD 39, 55, 112–13 n40; marijuana 39, 40, 46, 50, 57, 64, 102 n6
Dubini, Donatello and Fosco 5, 8; *Journey into the Mind of [P]* 5, 8
Dudar, Helen 45, 114–15 n50, 118 nn52–53, 123 n71, 132 n90

Dylan, Bob 8

Edmunds, Lowell 27
Eliot, T. S. 72
enclave 72, 73, 76, 78, 79, 86, 87, 93, 97
England 17, 46, 92, 116 n51
England, Barbara 115 n51
England, Jay Carter 115 n51
England, Norman 115–16 n51
entropy 92, 94, 95, 97, 100, 108 n25, 133–36 n92
Epoch 4
Ericson, Roky 9
Eisenhower, Dwight D. 122 n70
Esquire 112 n40

Fariña, Richard 5, 10, 19, 57, 72, 88–89, 90–91, 98, 106 n12, 113 n45, 124 n75; *Been Down So Long It Looks Like Up to Me* 19, 57, 88–89
feghoots 90
Feiffer, Jules 71, 124 n74; *Sick, Sick, Sick* 71, 124 n74
Ferlinghetti, Lawrence 28
Ford Foundation 69, 71–72, 123 n72
Freer, Joanna 36
Freud, Sigmund 83, 131 n86

Gable, John 127 n78
Gaddis, William 132 n89
Galvin, Kevin 123 n71
Ganz, Earl 23
Garcia Marquez, Gabriel 123 n73
Garfield, John 42, 67, 113 n41
Gary, Romain 87, 131 n89
Gebauer, Phyllis 25, 69, 109 n29
Gibbs, J. Willard 92
Ginsberg, Allen 28, 71, 86; "Howl" 71, 86
Glassow, Jonathan 115 n51, 123 n71
Gold, Herbert 106 n12
Goldwater, Barry 122 n70
Goodman, Irving 118 n52, 123 n71
Goodwin, Michael 5, 101 n4
Goolrick, Robert 105 n12
Gordon, Andrew 15–16, 107 n20
Grant, J. Kerry 120 n62

Hajdu, David 88, 91
Hall, Oakley 21; *Warlock* 21
"Harrigan" 84–85
Harrigan, Edward 84–85
Hayles, N. Katherine 49
He Ran All the Way 42
Herman, Luc 15, 93, 105 n12, 111 n35,

117–18 n52, 119 n57, 131 n88
"High Noon" 85, 86
Hill, Robert R. 36
Hillock, Bob 121–22 n70
hippies 26–27, 28, 35, 36, 38, 39, 41, 53, 112 n39
Hitchens, Christopher 116 n51
Hollander, Charles 80–81, 130 n84
Hudes, Karen 117 n52
Hyman, Stanly 89

Internet 8, 119 n61; ARPAnet 39; cyberspace 31

Jackson, Melanie 9, 46, 113 n46, 114 n49, 116 n51, 116–18 n52, 123 n71
jazz 82, 115 n51, 123 n72, 124 n74, 125 n78
John Larroquette Show 8–9
Johnson, Samuel 54

Kachka, Boris 12, 22, 34, 103 n9, 111 n36, 114 n50, 115 n51, 118 n53
Kakutani, Michiko 132 n89
Kennedy, John F., 10, 113 n45, 122 n70
Kerouac, Jack 28, 113 n41
Kesey, Ken 112 n40
Klein, William 25
Konstantinou, Lee 23
Krafft, John 8, 104 n10, 105 n12, 107 n13, 117 n52, 118 n53, 120 n63
Kramer, Larry 116 n51; *Faggots* 116 n51
Kristeva, Julia 31

Lane, Richard 8, 9–10, 12, 103 n8
Larroquette, John 8–9
Laufgraben, Lillian 103 n9
Leary, Timothy 40, 112 n40
Letzler, David 133–34 n92
Lippincott 11–12, 87, 103 n9, 105–6 n12, 107 n13, 109 n28
Lipson, Milton 121 n70
love 32, 47, 74–75, 77, 78, 79, 94–95, 110–11 n35, 129 n79, 130 n82, 134 n92
"Love for Sale" 95
Lud, Ned 41

Mahool, Patricia 71–72, 79, 103–4 n10, 105 n12
Malpas, Simon 97
Manson, Charles 29, 59, 112 n40
Martin, Justin 127 n78
Maschler, Tom 116 n51
Maxwell, Clerk 92

Maxwell's Demon 91, 92–93, 100
McCarthy, Cormac 9
McCarthy, Joseph 56, 58
McClintock, Scott 59
McHale, Brian 119 n56
Meindl, Dieter 51
Menand, Louis 113 n41
Mexico 6, 10, 31, 105 n11, 107 n18; Guadalajara 4; Mexico City 9–10
Milton, John 77, 78
Mirkowicz, Tomasz 113 n46
Mitchell, Daryl 9
Mizener, Arthur 91, 98
Monk, Thelonius, 137 n12
Morgan, Charley 7
Moses, Robert 14, 15
Mothra 43
Museum of Natural History 115 n51

New Leader 103 n9, 108 n26
New Dictionary of American Slang 120 n62
New World Writing 101 n4, 109 n28
New York 1, 14, 22, 45–46, 72, 73, 77, 79, 103 n9, 105–6 n12, 107 n19, 114 n49, 115 n50, 115–16 n51, 123 n71
New York Times 87, 131 n89
New York Times Book Review 51
Newsday 127 n78
Nixon, Richard 34–35,

Ochester, Edwin 101–2 n4
Orwell, George 50, 78–79, 110–11 n35, 120 n68, 130 n82; *Nineteen-Eighty Four* 78–79, 110–11 n35, 120 n68
Oswald, Lee Harvey 9–10
outlaw 48, 49–50, 63, 67
Ovid 135 n92

Paracelsus 135 n92
Parker, James 25
Patell, Cyrus R. K. 60
"Peggy Sue" 57
Penguin 7, 99, 107 n16
Phales 27
Plato 32
Plimpton, George 10
police 68, 112 n40; cop 63, 64, 66, 67
pop culture 85, 114 n50, 128 n78
Porush, David 49
promotional material 87, 131 n89; book trailer 7, 12–13, 15, 69, 99; t-shirts 7, 12–14, 99
Pseudo-Dionysius 28

publishing 9, 43, 104 n10, 113 n46
punctum 24, 25
Purple and Gold 79, 86
Pynchon, Jackson 1, 13, 102 n5
Pynchon, Judith 46, 118 n53
Pynchon, Thomas: Works: *Against the Day* 130 n84; *Bleeding Edge* 7, 12, 14–15, 22–23, 36–37, 39, 42, 62, 99, 108 n24, 119 n61; "Boys" 79–80, 86; *Crying of Lot 49* 4, 54–60, 68, 91–92, 113–14 n47, 117 n52, 131 n89, 132–33 n90; "Entropy" 13, 23, 92, 98, 99–100, 101 n3, 128 n78, 133–36 n92; *Gravity's Rainbow* 5, 15–16, 18, 44, 45, 46, 47, 90, 105 n12, 108 n20, 111 n35, 115 n50, 133 nn90–91; "Hallowe'en? Over Already?" 1–3, 101 n1, 102 n5; *Inherent Vice* 24, 25–33, 38–39, 40, 42, 46–47, 53–54, 59, 60–69, 71, 91, 110–11 n35, 119 n61; "Is It O.K. to Be a Luddite?," 41, 51, 114 n47; "Japanese Insurance Adjuster" 43, 44; "Journey into the Mind of Watts" 21, 38–39, 59, 66; "Low-lands" 101–2 n4, 109 n28; *Mason & Dixon* 44–45, 114 nn47–48; "Minstrel Island" 72, 72–79, 91, 124–30 nn75–81; "Mortality and Mercy in Vienna" 4, 101 n3; *Of a Fond Ghoul* 11, 104 n11; *Slow Learner* 50–51, 71, 90, 108 n21, 113 n46, 117 n52, 119 n61, 133 n92; "Small Rain" 14, 50, 79; "Under the Rose" 4, 101 n3; *V.* 3, 4, 11, 14, 23, 35, 45, 79, 87–88, 89, 101 n4, 103 n9, 104 n11; 105–6 n12; 108 n20; 109 n27, 112 n37, 114 nn48 and 50, 117 n52; *Vineland* 26, 29–30, 31, 33, 35–36, 39–41, 43–44, 46–49, 50, 51–53, 55, 56, 57, 60–61, 62–63, 66, 72, 86, 87, 110 n34, 119 nn58 and 61, 120–21 n68, 123 n71; "Voice of the Hamster" 79–85; "Ye Legend of Sir Stupid and the Purple Knight" 79–80, 81, 90
Pynchon Sr., Thomas 121 n70, 127 n78
Pynchon, William 15

recluse 13, 107 n18, 113 n42
Reese, Andrew 110 n30
Reich, Wilhelm 73
Reo, Don 9
Republican 28, 56, 68, 121 n70
Rink, Deane 3–5
Rock and Roll/Rock 'n' Roll 29, 40, 50, 56, 60; difference between "rock and roll" and "rock 'n' roll" 119 n61
Rockland Community College 115

Roeder, Bill 113 n44
Romanticism 69, 81, 128
Romney, George 121–22 n70
Roosevelt, Ethel 127 n78
Roosevelt, Theodore 127 n78
Rosenthal, Abe 51
Rowohlt 13, 99
Royster, Paul 101 n1
rumor 2, 3, 4–6, 7, 8, 10, 43, 44, 57, 82, 109 n28, 115 n50, 117 n52

Sale, Faith 6, 45, 87, 88, 90, 103–4 n10, 104 n11, 107 n18, 112 n37, 113 nn42 and 45, 115 n51
Sale, Kirkpatrick 22, 23, 45, 71–72, 73–79, 88, 90, 101 n4, 103 n9, 103–4 n10, 104 n11, 107 n18, 108 n26, 113 n45, 114–15 n50, 115 n51, 124 nn75–77, 124–30 nn78–81, 130 n83
Salinger, J. D. 7, 102 n5
Savage, Leonard J. 134 n92
Schaap, Dick 4
Seidler, David 10, 103 n9, 107 n13
Shannon, Claude E. 134 n92
Shetzline, David 10, 34, 42, 43, 45–46, 89–90, 115 n51, 133 n91
Siegel, Jules 10, 16, 101 n4, 102 n7, 112 n38
Silberman, James 105–6 n12
Silliman, Ron 5
Simon, Irving 136 n93
Simpsons 7
Sinatra, Frank 128 n78
Sinkler, Rebecca 51
Sixties (the cultural moment) 25, 28, 29, 33, 37, 39, 40–42, 46, 50, 51, 53, 59, 62, 113 n43
sixties (the decade) 5, 10, 16, 30, 34, 36, 40, 43, 53, 55, 102 n7, 104 n10, 113 n43, 120 n62
Slatoff, Walter 3–4
Smith, Corlies 11–12, 87–88, 103 n9, 103–4 n10, 104 n11, 105 n12, 107 nn14–15, 108 n27, 109 n28, 116 n51, 116–18 n52, 132 n90
Smith, Sheila, 116 n51
Sontag, Susan 24
Spigel, Lynn 55
St. Paul 27
Stalin 80
Staller, Karen M. 30
Star Trek 116 n51

Stencil [actual person], 108–9 n27
Stephens, Michael 43, 113 n46
Stevens, George 109 n28
Stewart, Jimmy 126 n78, 12 n78
Suez Crisis 109 n27
Suffolk Community College 118 n53

Taft, William Howard 121 n70
Tate, Sharon 112 n40
Taylor, Andrew 97
Television (TV) 7–8, 22, 33, 38, 39, 47, 55–56, 60, 67, 112 n39, 113 n41, 114 n50, 118 nn53–54, 119 n56
Texas 9–10, 40
Tharaldsen, Mary Ann 10, 12, 24, 34, 103 n9, 107 n18, 111 n36, 113 n45
Thompson, Hunter S. 40
Titanic 2
Tomaske, Stephen 8, 104 n10, 105 n12, 108 n27, 116 n51 116–17 n52, 123 n72
Trinidad 116 n51
Trotsky 80
Trotter J. K. 108 n24

Ulysses 87
USS Hank 108 n27

Veggian, Henry 107 n19
Vescovi, Gina Bria 1, 6
Viking 108 n20, 117 n52
Village Voice 124 n74

Wallace, David Foster 22, 46, 86–87, 108 n23, 131–32 n89; "Borges on the Couch" 108 n23; *Broom of the System* 131 n89; *Infinite Jest* 86–87, 131–32 n89
Warren Commission Report 103 n8
Wasserman, Harriet 105–6 n12, 117–18 n52, 133 n91
Weekend Sunday 132 n89
Weisenburger, Steven 15, 69, 91, 111 n35, 119 n57, 123 n72
Wexler, Chrissie 16, 69, 102 n7, 111 n36
Wideman, John Edgar 130 n85
Williamson, Edwin 22
Wilson Fellowship 4, 97
Winston, Mathew 3, 109 n28
Wisnicki, Adrian 103 n9
Who's Who 6

Yankee Doodle Dandy 84–85, 131 n87

www.ingramcontent.com/pod-product-compliance
Lightning Source LLC
Chambersburg PA
CBHW070944230426
43666CB00011B/2556